When HUGO *Meets* Shakespeare

When Hugo Meets Shakespeare: Volume 1

Copyright © 2022 by Jean René Bazin PierrePierre. All rights reserved.

ISBN: 979-8-9871406-0-4 (paperback)
         979-8-9871406-1-1 (ebook)

Printed in the United States of America

When *HUGO* *Meets* *Shakespeare*

Volume 1

Jean René Bazin PierrePierre

Table of Contents

Foreword

Well, there you go, good folks, right from Heaven's cascade,
A new genre of good read, your palate buds to raid.
It is not just poetry, not just classic poetry,
It's poetry with a swing, candid and yet sultry.
The writer has compiled, to make your dream come true,
A set of old favorites. Who would have thought it through?

Some feel they're déjà vu.
But still, they come brand-new,
With a bright Anglo tone
To sit on your hearts' throne.

He carried the genius, by the hand, lovingly,
Right across the channel, over to Lord Kingsley's.
There, amid famous teas, tasty biscuit choices,
He recorded keenly what poured from their voices.
The talks were so friendly around the hearth, at ease,
Hope so much the result, your loving hearts, will please.

And when French and English would clash, laden with pride,
When no one would back down, stubborn on either side,
He'd carefully sneak his imaginary clout
And settle any strife and erase any pout.
Twas such a daring task that his heart's still pounding
And his poor sanity, much shoved, is still dangling…
He carefully followed substance, footage, and rhyme
And transported them all over the span of time.
Again, he hopes so much you joined in the fairy.
For it's more than poetry, it's pure fiction poetry!

The Poet

Shakespeare ponders away, far from shiny Versailles,
Well-cut boxwoods and yews well trimmed and set thigh-high,
Right where tragedy groans, all weeping and verbose.
And he observed the crowd with fixed stare and then paused.

There, the woods all around shiver before his eyes.
Pale, he walks all dazzled, stunningly mesmerized.
He goes, fiercely and bold, and like a rusty mane,
Shaking off his forehead what shade of light remain'

From his translucent skull, full of corpses and souls,
Of dreams of which you see the bright glow to behold,
The whole world comes rolling and passes through his sieve.
He holds tight in his fist, life as it is conceived.

He makes his creatures cry with superhuman sobs.
He's this famous genius, who sheer sanity, robs.
Just like the somber sea which the mind, so baffles,
We capture, all trembling, what his theater stifles.

He rages on the mind with his breath astounding,
And the heart, his fingers ready to come wrenching.
And he never desists. He's a giant; he tames
Richard III or leopard, Caliban of huge frame.

The ideal is the wine poured by this dear Bacchus.
The monstrous, large subjects that he wrestles for us
Grumble all around him, splendid or misshapen.
He embraces Brutus, Lear, Hamlet with his pen,

Capulet, Montague, Caesar, and one by one,
The striges in the woods, the specter on the run
And after Aeschylus, and scaring Melpomene,
Sinister, holding up shreds of souls he demean',

Some flesh of Othello, some remains of Macbeth,
The drama of this work of unmeasurable depth,
And then he takes a rest. This lion of juggles
Falls asleep in his den with claws where blood dribbles.

Ibo

Oh! Tell me why, from what's hidden,
With great brass wall,
Deep within the celestial den
In blissful stalls,

Why in this great sanctuary,
Blessed and mute,
As wrapped in true mortuary
All absolute,

Conceal Your great eternal laws
And sound reasons
Since from you I will always draw,
Sole Perfection?

Why do you hide in the shadow,
Us to confuse?
Why do you ignore the sorrow
To You diffused?

That evil builds up or destroys,
Crawls or be king,
You know only You can employ
All my mind strings!

Chaste beauty, Ideal that befalls
Those suffering,
Who secures the mind rigid stalls
For hearts to sing.

You know too well, You I adore,
Love and Spirit,
You who dawns like ever before
And roams all streets,

Faith girdled of many bright stars,
Right owned by all,
I'll go seek Your truths near or far,
Heeding Your call!

For so long and with no boundary,
Bright rays of God,
Dwelled in your blessed heraldry,
Heavenly pod.

Soul seasoned to the great abyss,
From the cradle,
I always long for heaven's bliss.
My cage rattles!

Yes I'm a bird, like this creature
Amos dreamed of,
That St. Mark had noticed for sure
With eyes of love,

Who mingled its proudly raised top
To the radiance.
The eagle wing, over manes, drops,
Of lion stance.

I have wings; I yearn for the peak,
With flight secure.
I have wings even when storms wreak
The great azure.

I run up many countless steps;
I want to know.
Let science alone lose its pep,
Lost in shadow!

You know well that the soul faces
This strong desire,
That regardless of the races
I'll never tire!

You know well that the soul is strong
And has no fear.
When fed by God, it can't do wrong!
You know it, dear,

That I'll go till the pilasters
And that my steps
On the ladder, ever faster,
Never misstep!

In these troubled times, the creature,
In somber sea,
Prometheus and Adam mured,
What Eve could see.

He has to steal from the heavens
Th' eternal flame.
And conquer. And like the ravens,
Heist the great name.

He needs, deep within his cottage
By winds stricken,
A law that can tame any rage,
From life smitten.

From ignorance and misery,
In vain, man flees,
But fate commands and brings queries
At night he sees!

The people have to draw apart
From this decree,
And that at last, they come impart
All that they see!

Love shines upon the dark era,
Set to end soon,
Depicts the flickering aura
Of future moons.

On earth, the great laws of our fate,
God writes them down;
And if you ignore what they state,
I have the crown.

I am the unstoppable one,
The one who goes,
I am the ever-ready drone
Jehovah chose.

So I remain the one fierce poet,
Of chores laden,
The one poet of sorrow who yet
Has known disdain,

The dreamer who in his records
Puts the livings,
Mixing his stanzas in discord
With lyric strings,

The winged pensive, rough athlete
With agile arm,
Any comet I can defeat
Although disarm'.

So the laws of our dilemma,
I will have them.
I won't think about the trauma
Or where they stem!

Why keep these laws in deep secret?
Where there's no wall.
I though fire and sea upset,
Won't swerve at all.

I will go read the great Bible
All stripped and bare,
Deep in, where all is liable:
Thought, word, and stare,

Till the threshold of somber depths,
Gaping chasms
Where dwells the livid pack of death
In strong spasms,

Till the doors of visionaries
Of the heavens,
And if your thunder noise carries,
I'll roar and prance.

Lise

I was then twelve; she was sixteen years old,
And already was much taller than me.
So we can speak at night free of control,
I would wait until departs her mommy,
Then next to her I'd proudly take a seat
So I can open to her my spirit.

So many springs we lived amid flowers!
So many loves, in somber tombs, stifled!
Do we recall the mirth of love power?
Do you recall all the roses snuffled?
She once loved me; so did I. And we were
Two loving birds, growing up, free of lure.

God created her angel and princess.
Since she was older than me, I'd insist
On asking her questions, much more than less.
To make her talk, I just could not resist.
More than often, she would avoid my stare,
Afraid she was to size my childish care.

Then I'd show her all I knew as a boy,
My games and toys and my dear spinning top,
My Latin skills I was proud to deploy.
Phaedra, Virgil were not enough to stop
My bragging spree. I'd lie all upon her.
I'd even say, "My dad's an officer."

All together much often we would read.
In Latin verses, one gets often caught.
Sunday at church, I'd put her up to speed;
In tête-à-tête often we'd get distraught.
At my innocent plan, angels would smile
When we would read together for long while.

Of me she'd say, "He is only a child!"
And more often I would call her Ms. Lise.
Then one Sunday, a spring day, bright and mild,
A Latin psalm, the sense she could not seize,
In face-to-face, in attempt, O my Lord!
My burning lips stroke her cheek at its ford.

Sweet puppy love that faded away fast,
Clear dawning rays on my heart's budding lawn.
Enchant the youth, ecstasies of the past,
For much later your thrill will be all gone.
Bring back the trance to the bedazzled soul;
Sweet puppy love is never to unfold.

Solitude

So that's what solitude does to all human beings.
She reveals God to them, unveils all sacred things
From the world still hidden.
She fills up with splendor the one, who comes to probe,
And from within the depths of what their dreams enrobe,
The truth comes out brightened.

She feeds the ignorant the enormous science:
What the great cedar sees, the elm sweet defiance,
And what the oak perceives.
God, the creature, the space, eternity and such,
The abyss, all mingled to candor that won't lurch
Of a herder, love deaves.

She finds him a mere lamp, yet she makes him a star.
And this herder becomes, under his rags thus far,
A king; and then at times,
To the flower essence, the trees, the pilasters,
He appears with tiara, like a real-life master
Glowing in this new lime!

He does not have a doubt of this subtle grandeur:
Seated by his fire fed by shrubs of duster,
Hails the Supreme Being.
Humble, he thinks, puny and meek and quite lifeless.
He bends down, and there feels, sizing his nothingness,
The size of his being.

At the end of his dream, he goes back to nature.
He sweet- talks to the brume, along its adventure,
Sipping from the azure.
He says, "What chaste essence, you spread, O my dear mist!"
He says to the dear bird, "Say, how can you resist
The winds with such stature?"

At night, when he sees one walk toward the village,
Gleaners or lumberjacks, dragging useful foliage,
With hard working horses,
Stricken by the sower, prey of bouts of anger,
Not knowing his brother, from waves gets back sluggers,
Battling sea wind forces.

When he sees the convicts carrying their burdens,
The soldiers, fishermen rushing back to their dens,
In the dead of the night,
He sends to everyone from up the somber mount
The blessing he received from the eternal font
Of love's impressive might.

And while he remains there upon this quiet hill,
Contented and bowing before all that instill
In him this peaceful air,
Flowing through the small vale, the field, the mossy roof,
The grass, and the big stone, all of deep love, the proof
Fit for his heart's affair.

If ever comes around, nearing his inner peace,
One of these great spirits, fed up with cowardice
That in the world he sees,
Who fear altogether upon these somber waves
The earth of pure granite and sky of star unpaved,
Man ingrate, God deceived

Maybe, without a sound, that this peaceful herder,
Who in spite of darkness glows of a light fonder,
Naturally contented,
Perceived by this lost soul, tossed around by the waves,
Will reveal suddenly, through the bright light that saves,
The shores so pretended.

And maybe this fire, against this somber rock,
From far away noticed by a boat in havoc
Between the sea and sky,
Humble, he will show it, with its bright-amber gleam,
The way and as it warms the herder with its steam,
Will help the boat sail by.

While Knocking at a Door

I lost my father and mother.
Alas! My first-born went so young.
For me nature never smother',
Always tolled strong.

I slept between my two brothers;
We were like three birds as children.
Alas! Fate changed in pall covers
Their cribs of then.

I lost you, O my dear daughter,
You who filled up, O vain estate,
My destiny with the luster
Of your pine crate.

I did ascend and did descend.
In my world, I knew dusk and dawn.
The purple and ash scary trend
That my life spawns.

I have known profound eagerness;
I have known morose love affairs.
I have seen fly all loveliness
Far from my care.

Above my head I have a sword.
Against my work, I have envy;
I have pitfalls, inner discords,
Thoughts much heavy.

My teary eyes are thoughts laden;
My garments are shred in the cold.
Nothing else fancies my heart, then.
I am here, scaffold!

Nomen, Numen, Lumen

And when it was all done, when the stars all scattered,
Dazzled by the chaos, from all corners chattered,
Finally took their place in the vast universe,
God felt the surging need, on it, His name, to verse
And the sublime Being stood up, ever serene,
Uttered loud, "Jehovah" over his treasured scene.
And in the great abyss, these seven letters rolled
And formed in the deep sky, that with keen eyes we scroll,
All above our heads, trembling under their shine,
The seven giant stars set on the northern vine.

To a Poet

My friend, eclipse your life and open your spirit,
This mound where the good grass grows up from your merit,
Ravines from where emerge grazing goats from trenches,
A peaceful vale hidden under somber branches,
Ideal for birds to nest, with subtle voice murmurs,
Where the breeze comes causing flickering apertures,
Like a sequin beset by some unknown fairy,
Rays of sun, here and there, to make your soul merry.

A few rocks, by heaven, placed all around wisely
Just to cause soft echoes deep in the woods fondly,
This should be your domain, the place where you evolve!
That there, around your hearth, they sing, laugh, cry, and love.
Tis where you should remain. Make it your lovely den,
Barely making a sound to disclose the hidden.
While introspecting, you discover deep within
The life free of burden with time still and lasting.

Then again, when you glance, all so lightheartedly,
The children physically, the dead spiritually!
And then at the same time, around the world, by chance,
August and vagabond, depending on her stance,
Far from and right above your gleamy horizon,
Let erupt your poetry straight to the rising sun!
In the raucous cities, as in peaceful meadows,
Fondled along its way by the living shadows,

Allow her to hover, ever-shining crystal,
And fly toward heaven, source of bliss eternal.
Calm and pure all around, the souls of her enriched,
An immense living flow of words to ideas stitched,
Which collects on its way in this majestic stream
Any brook from the earth or ponds of blissful themes!
You, bask in the shadows! And ignoring your life,
In blessed quiescence, reverend, free of strife,
Remain in the background as a mysterious mind!

That the lone traveler, affected, comes to find,
Driven by pure hazard at the steps of your door,
Relief for his parched lips, hope to strengthen his core,
Courage for his journey and solace on the road
And quench his weary soul from your font and upload,
Just like the rest of them, in need of condolement.
Remain meek like a brook, yet roar like a torrent!

Dreams

I

Friends, away from the town,
Far from all palaces,
Away from courting frown,
Far from where people drown,
Come, follow the traces

Of meadows where the soul
Can laze in a dreamland
On a shore free of toll
And of noise as a whole,
With the breeze and sand,

And some beaten down shed,
Old but with sturdy walls.
A dock where one can tread,
A nest the tree can't shed,
A manor with long halls

That'd be calm and somber,
Peaceful and relaxing,
With trees in great number,
A giant in slumber,
Well-hidden from all things,

That there, bracing it all,
Not deceiving any,
My rhyme runs from its stall
Toward a river fall
Or tree-bird harmony.

That it would dare to soar,
Free from the least of snare
High in the sky to roar
And the heavens, explore
Like a bird, free of care.

II

That in dreams, I remain
Full of loving shadows,
That the steady refrain
Echoes on the terrain
Days and nights in a row!

Like the silvery veil
In the far horizon
That to a star avail,
It glides there to unveil
Souls in sheer unison!

That my dear muse who dwells
And kindles all my nights
Make it glow and dispel
All that can, like a bell,
Wake me from its delight.

That the flow of my thoughts
Comes raging deep within,
Clinging to what they brought,
What at so much they wrought
Of my innermost scene.

That all bound to my dream
They, with bright, gleaming eyes,
Cradle its treasured themes,
Holding them in esteem,
Like their most precious prize.

III

Deep within the forest
Or on the mountaintop,
As long as we're at rest
With nothing on the chest,
In jovial glee we hop.

And we cradle the dream
Where every spoken word
Is a melodious scream,
From the wave steady theme
To the softest breeze heard.

And the echo resounds
Deep within the whole world,
Like the globe's inner ground,
A universal sound
That from the sea would swirl.

It's the blessed echo
Ringing out from heavens;
From all the hosts it flows
To this world down belo
Where life keeps up its prance,

Ignoring the clamors
Of all that can be voiced.
Soul to soul gives candor,
Flame restores flame ardor,
And the sea waves rejoice.

IV

This clamor always soars
From all over the lands
And, like never before,
Touches the earth's decor
Down to the least of strands.

Even in foreign plains
Or foamy, rocky mounts
Or, setting the same train,
A dungeon that'd sustain
Of them a steady count

Where the center tower,
The choice place for my laze,
Will wear, as sole flower,
Some ivy that'd tower
Its facade all-ablaze.

As long as well adorned
Of a much haughty shield,
With hearth that can't be scorned,
All gaping, set to dawn,
A mighty oak would yield.

That in the warm summer
Would conceal my blue dome,
In winter makes glimmer,
Avoiding the grimmer
Aspects of my sweet home.

In the woods, my kingdom,
If at night, all buzzing,
Make that when near, they come,
They see heads of phantoms
Glow and shadows dancing!

And that some virgin bees
Stirring the somber vault,
My concerns come appease,
Shaking as though they tease,
Their wings with sudden volts.

And that with mourning sound,
All the heroes of old
Come sneakily around,
Display their floating pounds
At the forest threshold.

V

But if my muse decides
To dip my craving mind
In treasures that abide
In some maze, I won't chide
Her, but treading behind

And truly mesmerized,
I'll delight at her choice
For being my favorite prize.
I cherish all the ties
With this era much poised.

Often when the strong wing
Displaces the swallow,
She uncovers new strings
And hatches her offspring
In vultures' tree burrow.

There, the brood tenderly,
Ignoring the venture,
Playfully breaks slowly
The egg of the ugly
And ferocious vulture.

And so facing the risk
Daring my sanity,
My rhyme will come and frisk
With search frantic and brisk
Those old castles bounty.

Then wrapped in greenish vine,
My days will shine aglow
With rhyme of solid spine,
Dressed up just to define
Blessed joy or sorrow.

Be it dungeon or shed,
I'll be free of all ties
With soul silently fed
By Zion's precious bread
Under God's watchful eyes.

Evening Stroll

So don your lovely shawl matching your eyes so well.
You know the very one; you can easily tell,
Goes with everything that you wear.
It's classy and silky, of such a rare fabric,
That even to the blind, with it, you're fantastic
And draw to you every one's stare.

See the many hamlets as the sun comes to set,
With smoky domes alike, that their long day, offset,
Just like the troubles we ferry.
We all transport a torch as weak and flickering hope
And like the last sunrays down that green amber slope
That far from us time comes carry.

At this time when the sun tells the mounts its goodbyes,
How lucky can I be to still see in your eyes
The glow that brings the world such cheer!
How sweet it's to embrace the magic of this time;
When free of any gloom, I can display my prime
And proudly show you around, dear!

It's to live such moments that I forsook all things,
That I simply remained, all my life, suffering
All that you know I bore before.
I want to offer you a world peaceful and free.
No more of loneliness, we'll live and be merry,
With blessings from heavens galore.

Every now, every then, in that glittering dome,
A star shines right out loud like pure celestial chrome,
To shed its light in someone's heart.
And much more than often, at the end of the night,
Nature at its darkest meets a dawn clear and bright,
Joy or sorrow, to us impart.

Hey, see that meteor; it shines bright then goes off.
So did many great men, at whom the world now scoffs.
They shine, then to the tomb they go.
The average man follows, led by their senseless bang.
The hard worker always will disregard the prang
Done on its turf long time ago.

But you're not like the rest. You care deeply for those
Who traverse hardship yet remain with their white clothes,
Working safely on their heaven.
You victim-advocate and pray for the guilty,
Being so well-imbued of life's blessed frailty
And how people can be driven.

If ever in your way arise somber hurdles
Designed to throw you off while you safely straddle
The goal you set your mind upon,
You pause for a short while; and ever graciously,
You redesign a plan and then feverishly
Proceed to better horizon.

I instilled deep in you this choice of diversion;
It is always helpful in any dimension.
This world is full of surprises.
Even the lonely poet, scribbling, taking a nap,
When around comes his muse to gently his soul, tap,
He only swiftly arises.

But let's go home, my dear; the shadows found the earth,
Leave them to their embrace; I'll settle for your mirth,
To me the most precious reward.
Life offers you chances; grab a hold and pretend
It's your last day of life, so take her by the hand
And around all else, disregard.

Every given minute cements your destiny;
The body, from the soul, suffers sheer mutiny,
The end result of this here life.
Live as to not regret, live to your soul, protect
From flagrant defaulters and willful disrespect,
Denouement of most inner strife.

Blessed be the Child

From all the blazing suns, the planets, and the stars,
Shimmering palaces with ajar golden gates,
From all the beaming rays and sacred veils that are
Floating gently deep in all states!

In the deep sea of love drowning our very soul,
Source of the fiery, great seraphim's arrow,
The non-ending spinning around the throne of gold
Of this globe's incandescent glow!

Amid the many games of relentless children
Under the caring eye and vigilant retort
Of this genie of old with long and sturdy reins,
Watching the least of their efforts,

Or that some lovely dame raving under their charms
Imprints on their forehead the softness of a kiss,
That basking and cooing in her so loving arms,
They reveal their infantile bliss,

That finally, gliding in His celestial ark,
Throughout His friendly skies with His angels in tow,
The good Lord, repeating one of His greatest marks,
Would place them around Him in row.

From the everlasting charms of joyful azure
Amid the sheer goodness, free of the least sorrow,
Child, apart from the look of mother so demure,
Don't you miss heavens' blissful glow?

The Giant

Listen, O warriors, I'm from the land of Gauls;
My ancestors, lively, crossed the Rhine like a brook.
My mother immersed me in the snow of the poles,
And upon his shoulders, my father often hauled
Grizzlies and used their skins to decorate my nook.

He was strong, the old man, but now he's declining.
His face is all furrowed, and his hair is all gray.
He is weak and feeble, and his end is looming.
He can hardly uproot an oak, among all things,
To help him walk along the way.

I am here in his stead; I hold his javelin.
Of all he once possessed, all belongs to me now.
I who can easily, his footsteps falling in,
Sit high on the mountain, feet in the vale, resting,
And with one breath of mine can make the poplars bow.

When I was a young man, in the Alps, in the woods,
Agile and quick leaping, I trail-blazed rocks and hills.
As tall as a mountain, my head through clouds protrude'
And there, scanning the skies, caught all eagles I could;
This gave me always such a thrill.

With the sound of my breath, I could top the thunder
And, with an even snap, cut the lightning fizzle.
Or even playfully, the waves stirring under,
I chased the mighty whales and from the seas plunder'
The deep hidden treasures, with pirates bedazzled.

I roamed and chased away, in all the deep waters,
The sharks, the octopus, and predators alike.
I could choke hold a bear with my arms or batter
Their snowy daylight out, stop their growling chatter.
Scare the wolves way behind their dikes.

Those old teenage pass time have lost all interest;
Now I find much appeal in wars and manly games.
The calamity prongs, the familial unrests,
The camps and the soldiers, always fit to contest,
Chasing some senseless thrill, along with senseless fame.

Deep into the bloodshed in the fiercest combat,
When the skirmish excels in much heated onslaught,
That's when I dive headfirst, with or without a bat,
Just like the cormorants when their main meal they spot,
Between the wavy waters caught.

And liking a reaper amid the ripen sheaves
In the rows all trampled, I stand alone, erect.
No more fighting clamor, pure murmur I retrieve.
I pummel here and there, eager not to deceive
My underfed frenzy and boasting self-respect.

I walk around naked and crack up at the sight
Of the iron soldiers of which you are so proud.
I take my wooden spade in the most of my fights,
Along with my helmet, so subtle and so light
But can put strong bulls in the clouds.

I don't waste any time escalating ladders;
I break their portal chains when invading their forts
And tumble down their walls just like a ram batters
And wrestle their towers, ignoring the blatter
Of the great many folks; they shield from my efforts.

But when my time will come, like for all my victims,
Warriors, don't permit birds on my carcass to feed.
Lay my body to rest, to lofty mountains, trim,
That amid their high peaks, to the stranger it'd seem,
Of this here life, how much I greed.

The Phantoms

I

Alas! How numerous the maidens I saw die!
Sad fate! Death has to claim its quota of victims.
All by the dreaded scythe, plenty of grass now lie;
Always in jolly balls, when the quadrilles come by,
Roses are crushed in silent screams.

The quenching waters flow in vales till there's no more;
The startling lightning shines, shining for just a while.
The envious April with sudden freeze will bore
The blooming apple tree, with springtime in its core,
Bragging its renewed style.

Well, c'est la vie! After the day, the hollow night.
After all comes the dawn, troublesome or jolly.
At the great feast table, with meals heavy or light,
So many invited disappear of all sights
Way before the final tally.

II

The many I saw die! There was the pink and white.
The other seemed to bask in blissful harmony,
Yet the other, feeble, would rest her head a slight.
Just like the swallow bends the branch before its flight,
Her soul played a last symphony.

Another, pale and lost, under heavy burden,
Kept repeating a name that no one remembers.
Another passed out like a muted refrain,
And a third, expiring, smiled as a sweet maiden
Seeing an angel that slumbers.

All of them fragile pearls set with early demise!
Halcyons quickly drowned in tumultuous waters!
Doves from heaven bequeathed to woefulness chastise,
Bearer of innocence and of grace, flagrant prize,
Who'd gladden souls with their laughter.

But they all departed, lying in the cold tomb!
All so lovely maidens carried over the Styx!
All these smothered beacons, all roses that succumb'
Ah! Let me stroll gladly deep in the forest womb
And enjoy my fallen leave fix!

Lovely ghosts! It's right here; when I leap to their sphere
That inquisitively, one by one they come meet.
And though I don't perceive in their eyes any tear,
From their graceful shadow and the way that they peer,
They had a too-early exit.

My soul remains bonded to all those lovely mates.
And life and the cold tomb lost their early power.
At times I walk along, condoling in their fate,
Taking in earnestly the full weight of their plate,
Just midst them to pass the hour.

And to my every thought they lend and shape and form.
I see them so clearly when comes the eventide.
They come around the tomb and make a gentle storm,
Dancing around a while to easily transform
My every dusk in dreamy slides.

III

One of them. - An angel, a lovely Spanish girl!
Silky hands, breast engorged by long innocent sighs,
With brown eyes all aglow, like the loveliest pearl,
With such a foreign charm underneath her dark curls
That would cascade down to her thighs.

She did not die of love at such an age. For her
Love had not bloomed as yet, neither its thorn nor rose.
No Don had succeeded to make her surrender.
Well aware of her charm, she spoiled no contender,
Whether they spoke in rhyme or prose.

But she loved to party, and that caused her downfall.
The peppery parties, the ones that would not end.
She still moves in her tomb at the sound of a ball;
Even deep in the night, mainly in early fall,
Catch her mist dancing now and then.

She was so addicted! An upcoming party
Would send her in a trance that in her mind would hide;
She would dream it over, losing serenity.
Musicians and dancers would rob her sanity,
Laughter and brawls at her bedside.

Then there were the glitters, jewels, and ornaments,
The lovely moiré belts with undulant designs,
The rarest of dresses of the lightest garments,
Bright festoons and ribbons over walls and pavements,
Flowers at every hooks and signs.

When the party would start, giggling with her siblings,
She'd run all elated, with her fan in her hand.
She would sit in the midst of the silk scarfs, gloating,
With her heart quivering, right in the band playing
All pieces that were in the trend.

Twas such a joy to sit and watch this young girl dance!
Her skirt would fly around, flinging its blue sequins.
Her doe-eyes all aglow, revealing lively trance,
Shined like a double star over the dome of France,
In the dark sky scintillating.

She was bursting of joy, of giggle, and of pep.
We would just watch her dance. What a pleasure that was!
For she was natural, genuine in every step;
She would quickly unwind while the rest of us slept.
Far from this, she'd go bananas!

She would sway in a waltz or enter in a swing,
All carried by the thrill without taking a break.
All intoxicated by the noise glittering,
By the flowers galore, the lights, and the giggling
Amid footsteps and booty shake.

But what a thrill it was to jump right in the crowd,
To melt and feel the zest of joy burst from the chest!
To forget all worries, all troubles put in shroud.
To dismiss every ache, blocking all with the loud
And jovial feel within your breast.

But alas! Everything has to come to an end.
And you have to exit in the fresh dawn and wait
That they bring you your coat. That's where the cooling hand
Of the caressing chill, she failed to comprehend,
Impressed on her the deadly fate.

If only the party knew the sad tomorrow
Devoid of all laughter, of giggle, and of dance!
When hacking cough steps in, swimming in your sorrow,
You forget the hit tunes. The fever steals the glow
Of those doe-eyes' once jolly trance.

IV

And she died! At fifteen, happy, treasured, lovely!
Right after the party and we were all surprised.
She died within the arms of her mother slowly,
Carried all dressed to dance but with Charon only
Lying in a box made her size.

So she went on dancing but with flying partners;
That's how fast she was flown into the world of hosts.
And the many roses, held on by fasteners,
In her coffin followed, changing their demeanor.
Now she goes entertaining ghosts.

V

Her poor mother all crushed, ignorant of her fate,
After all this cradling for this fragile willow,
After the many wakes over her childhood state
And the so many tears poured over at the gate
Of her younger years in a row.

But now she is no more. Beautiful, gone too soon,
Inert in the cold tomb slowly turning to dust
Rests now eternally. Unless in some full moon,
Some party for the dead, enclosed deep in her toon,
Wakes her up in a dancing thrust.

A spook with dreadful laugh attends to all her needs;
Like a caring mother, it says, "The time is now!"
And on her blueish lips, after its dire deeds,
Impresses a cold kiss then, bereft of all speed,
Fixes her long black hair somehow.

Then all shaky, walks her to the macabre dance,
Where, in the crimson sky and the dancing shadow,
The moon takes on a glow, gray and pale in outrance,
The night rainbow shows up in heaven defiance,
The thunder roars in faint echo.

VI

All you girls, party pearls, all enthralled by this thrill,
Think about that poor girl, gone to never come back.
Young ladies, yes, she was happy-go--lucky till
The last night so fatal, preceding her fall ill.
She had all going on her track!

The poor kid went around from party to party,
Spreading lovely roses wherever she would land.
But how sad it still is that she went so pretty,
So young, and so precious in all nitty-gritty…
She died with flowers in her hands.

The Jinns

Walls, town,
And quay
All down
Like slay'
Sea bare
Where tears
The air
All gray.

The meadows
Birth a sound.
Somber glow
On the ground.
From a bawl
Soars a call
At nightfall
That rebounds.

The loudest noise
Favors sleigh bell.
A dwarfing poise
Runs in to quell
But jumps, dances,
And then prances,
Seeking chances
Around the well.

The rumor's nearing;
The echo repeats.
Its bell has the ring
Of a damned retreat.
Like a rolling crowd
That thunders out loud,
It dies in a shroud
Then finds an exit.

God! The guttural voice
Of jinns! What a racket!
Come quick, we have no choice.
Let's hide in the closet!
My oil lamp is dying,
And the shadows, crawling,
Are getting more startling,
Such a macabre set.

A swarm of jinns passing by,
Whirling and whistling along,
Shaking the yews as they fly
That they crack as though not strong.
Swiftly goes their heavy flock
In the night sky to unlock
All the clouds within the block,
Setting lightning in the throng.

They're getting close, so keep airtight
This room in which we're teasing them.
What noise they make! Angels of fright
From which vampires and dragons stem!
The roof frame rattles more and more
And resounds deep within its core.
And the steel hinges of the door
Are giving in to the mayhem.

Clamors from hell! Howling and crying loud!
Horrible swarm! Voices blown by the winds
That with no doubt come falling from the clouds
Over my house whose walls sound now so thin.
The house trembles within its foundation,
And it appears, like horror flick action,
To whirl and jump in strong repetitions
Like a dead leaf that the summer wind spins.

O prophet! If you can save me
From this swarm of demons of night,
I will go bow, meek and clammy
My forehead before your great might!
Make sturdy the hinges of steel
And do not allow that they steal
Of your faithful the treasured seal!
Their daring assaults come and smite!

They went right by! Their cohort
Flew by and fled, and their feet
Stopped stomping now to abort
The strike they dared to repeat.
In the air they left the trace
Of the stench fit to their race.
On their way now, they'll debase
Forest trees in their retreat.

You can hear the decrease
Of their flapping of wings,
Still faint as they release
Their howl and bawling strings.
You can hear the insects
Caught as they interject
To this storm they reject,
Troubling their humble ease.

Some strange syllables
Still come to our mind,
Making us able
When it's time to find
A rest for the soul
And a chance to hold
All that we were told
From when we were kind.

The woeful jinns,
Death begotten,
Carry their sins
Back to their den.
They swarm aloud,
But in their shroud,
Their size of crowd
None can attain.

This vague noise
Dying out
Has a poise
Of mute shout.
It's the moan
Almost gone
But well known
To death snout.

No doubt
At night,
All shout
Strikes fright.
All foes
Go low
Although
They bite.

Fragments of the Serpent

Awake all day, all night, I feverishly dream,
Drowning in bitter tears,
Since my Albaydé, her sight forever dimmed
In the tomb for all years.

She was only fifteen, with a most candid smile,
Of me, truly in love,
And when over her breast, her arms she'd cross a while,
Angels cooed from above!

One day, in thoughts drifting, I came across a bay
Between two capes, dormant,
And saw green and yellow on the sand where it lay,
A black spotted serpent.

In so many fragments, an ax had cut, alive,
Its body sea-awash,
And every foamy wave that the tide chose to drive
Would turn in pink panache.

Every bloody fragment wiggled relentlessly
On the deserted strand,
And the blood steadily would bathe repeatedly
A ridge upon the sand.

These sections thrown apart, life slowly abating,
Wearing themselves away,
For last farewell kiss were one another searching,
All writhing on their way.

But since I was dreaming, begging God and all sad,
In my pitiful plea,
The head of thousand teeth opened its eye a tad
And to me, these words flee:

"Poet, pity yourself! Your lot is much it seems,
Worst off remains your prize!
Now that Albaydé chose forever to dim,
In the tomb, her doe-eyes.

"This ax that came destroy your pristine soar as well
Your whole world tears apart.
Your life and all your thoughts, as down in a deep well,
Bleed from this woeful dart.

"Your spirit flying high sparkly and gracefully,
Better than a swallow,
Over mounts and meadows or the sky overtly
Soaring where the winds blow,

"Just like me, lies stifling upon this sandy shore,
Too reluctant to sway,
Unable to rejoin his fragments as before,
Bleeding his life away."

Nourmahal, the Redhead Girl

Amid those rocks of ebony,
Do you see that somber thicket
That springs among the so many,
Like a forest of Albany,
Between two mounts of Nantucket?

There, deep inside the clear shadow
Growls the wounded yellow tiger,
The lioness roars in echo,
The jackal, the hyena show,
And the leopard not so meager.

There, crawl monsters of any form,
Of any aspect known to men.
The hippopotamus that storms,
And the boa, not in the norm,
That never leaves any remain.

The goldfish with ruddy eyelids,
The serpent and the mean monkey
That whistles like a swarm that speeds.
The elephant always morbid
With its demeanor so low-key.

There lives the savage family,
Where we yelp, buzz, and then bellow.
The whole forest becomes lively.
Under each thicket, lovingly,
Every action has its echo.

So on the moss, naked alone,
It's Nourmahal, the redhead girl.
She looks so lovely on her throne.
There, as she plays with the pinecones,
At her feet you can put the world.

The Curse

Let him roam aimlessly, laden from early on
Where the sunrays smolder the fleeting horizons,
And not one cloud wander!
Like a dark murderer fleeing deep in the night,
If he's walking that he, from the shadows that smite,
Hears footsteps in thunder!

On slippery glaciers, thin as a cutting ax,
That he slips and tumbles, falls and rolls, and then grasps
With teeth and nails its walls!
That mistakenly he'd be captured and tortured,
Nailing him on a cross and that with no measure,
"I'm innocent!" he bawls!

That he hangs, all haggard, with cyanotic lips!
That death comes sneakily, his living light, eclipse'
Coldly shriek and jeering!
That even dead, he still suffers enough to feel
Death gnawing at great bites his cadaver and still,
Slowly his skin peeling!

That no longer alive, of soul he'd be devoid,
That on his naked skin hot sunrays be deployed
Or torrential deluge!
That he wakes up startled every night in the wild,
And he fights desperately, choking on bitter bile,
In vain seeking refuge!

The Dervish

One day, Ali went by, and the highest degrees
Bowed down in reverence from all his pedigree.
And everyone would scream, "Allah!"
Suddenly a dervish, heavily year-laden,
Dashed through the crowd and took his horse right by the rein
And said to him, as good fellah,

"Ali-Tepelena, O you, light of all lights,
Who sits upon the throne, well-endowed with all might,
Whose name is blessed forever,
Hear me, O you vizier of many war heroes,
Great Padishah shadow that God overshadows,
You're but a forsaken beaver!

"A sepulchre torch leads your flagrant ignorance.
Like an over-flown vase, you spill your annoyance
Upon your quivering nation.
You lord it over them like a scythe over grass.
You crush mercilessly, with all that you amass,
Their lives beyond all compassion!

"But you'll get yours. For thus, in the old Janina,
Your upcoming demise has gained in stamina!
God chose you an iron bridle
Deep into the segjin, amid the godless souls,
Scattered on the dark soil, freezing beyond control,
In seventh hell somber girdle!

"Your naked soul will flee! When upon you will rush,
Right from the book of hell, all those crimes that you hushed,
They'll be called to your ears.
Those ghosts ever craving your lifeless soul to tear
Will never hear the sound of the mumble you'll dare
Voice out, lost in your deep fears!

"This surely will happen, and not your strong fortress
Or your large fleet will help in your distress
Or steer away this disaster.
Even Ali-Pasha, like the forsaken Jew,
To dupe the dark angel, eager to get his due,
Before dying would turn pastor!"

Ali in his pelisse harbored a scimitar,
A loaded short musket, with mouth like a crater,
Three long shot guns, and a bleeder,
In silence heeds the priest, right to the very end,
Bent over thoughtfully, calmly smiled at him, and
Gave his pelisse to the elder.

The Favorite Sultana

Haven't I, for you, Jewish girl,
Almost emptied my whole harem?
Allow the rest to show their curls.
Every night, you don't have to hurl
Unfounded suspicions at them.

Relax yourself, my young mistress.
Be kind to the other ladies.
You are my most precious princess.
Your lovely soul, don't let them stress;
They're just a bunch of nobodies.

Desist from chewing on these thoughts;
Your kindness freely will flow through.
Toward you my concerns are brought,
And I can assure you that naught
Will ever come 'tween me and you.

Of jealousy, you are the queen!
So beautiful with heart of steel!
To the others don't be so mean.
No garden flower has been seen
Wither next to the rose appeal.

Am I not all yours? Then who cares,
When we lie here in sweet embrace,
If all the others, in despair,
Envy your eyes and your long hair,
Exquisite showcase of your race.

In their distressing solitude,
Let them all boil in silent rage.
Just bask in the beatitude
And toward them don't be so rude.
You have my heart in your sweet cage.

All that I have I give to you,
My whole kingdom and Istanbul,
City where all the dreams come true,
Shining in the bay, as the new
Beacon of hopes for the faithful.

To you only and no other,
My devoted spahis daily.
Run to attend and to smother
Any trouble that would bother.
Your blue eyes I revere mostly!

To you Basra and Trebizond,
Cyprus, with its old names engraved,
Fez, with its golden powder ponds,
Mosul, to which the world responds,
Erzurum, with its streets all paved!

To you Izmir, with new houses,
Where the waters come all awash!
Ganges, the nightmare of spouses,
Danube whose river arouses
Five streams, the great ocean to wash!

Do you fret about the Greek girls?
The pale lilies of Damanhur?
The fiery glow of the black pearls,
With piercing eyes and coarse black curls,
With strong love and subtle power?

Does it matter, my Jewish dove,
Ebony breast or cherry tint?
You're not white, but nothing can shove
The complexion that from above,
The sun itself on your skin prints.

So from now on, calm your fury,
Jewess, on all the poor flowers,
Enjoy peacefully the cherry.
No need to mentally scurry,
Trying to secure your power.

Focus only on the plane trees,
On the many warm scented baths,
On the tartans gliding so free…
A sultan has sultana spree
As daggers sow death on their paths.

The Pasha's Sorrow

"What's with Allah's shadow?" Said the humble dervish.
His alms are so meager, yet his treasures are rich!
Stingy, somber, stagnant, with a bitter laughter.
Has he chipped by mistake the sword of his father?
Has he, of his soldiers, all hither than thither,
Perceived the thunderous cluster?

"What's with the dear pasha, vizier of all armies?"
Uttered all the gunners, with wicks lite and gleamy.
Have imams disrupted this iron-cast forehead?
Of blessed Ramadan, has he broken the fast?
Has he seen in a dream, passing swift, passing fast,
The angel Azrael, watching Hades with stead?

"What's wrong with him?" Pondered the stupid icoglans.
Did they say that he lost the complicated plans
Of the vessel of oils of everlasting youth?
Will they, in Istanbul, find his age-old glory?
Was he given some news so premonitory,
Oracle of tomorrow's truth?

"What's with the meek sultan?" Wondered the sultanas.
Has he caught with his son, he would go bananas,
His favorite sultana with lips juicy and red?
Have they put in his bath some sleazy aroma?
In the fellah's satchel, Allah saves from drama,
Is the harem missing a long-expected head?

"What's wrong with the master?" Inquire all the slaves.
They are all wrong. Alas! If so, lost for his braves,
Seated as a warrior suffering an affront,
Bent over just as if, all crushed under the years,
For three days and three nights, he really could not veer
From all those thoughts he now confronts.

It's not that he had seen the infidel revolt
Besieging his harem, his most precious of forts,
Throw in his cozy bed some candescent ember,
Or that a forefather would be waving a sword
Or that Azrael show up or that, bound up in cord,
He'd seen his motley mutes sweating in his slumber.

Alas! Allah's shadow did not break any fast,
The sultana's guarded, and his son's crawling fast,
No vessel came to shore from some stormy burden
The Tartar still reeled in its quota as before,
The harem was complete, with muttered sighs galore.
Nothing's amiss this precious den.

It is neither question of the fallen cities
Nor of human remains, free-roaming entities
Nor old Greece burning down by the sons of Omar,
The orphan all-alone, the widow's bitter wail,
Nor the butchered childhood when parents can't prevail
Nor the crude auctioning of virgins in Thamar.

No, it's not a question of these mournful subjects,
With all the driving prongs they bring in retrospect,
When they glide on his soul, drowning in its remorse.
What's wrong with this pasha who should be waging war,
Who, so sad and gloomy, weeps like a movie star...?
His Nubian tiger, death endorsed.

Enthusiasm

To Greece! To Greece! Farewell, you all! We got to go!
It's about time, after the honest blood they sow,
That those butcher blood we now spill!
To Greece, O my dear friends! Revenge and liberty!
With my turban around and my saber ready,
Come on! Get my horse in the thrill!

When is it, already, that we're leaving? It's late!
Some weapons, some horses, and a rapid frigate!
I wish so much we could just fly!
Let's take along with us whatever regiment
Is left, and we'll notice the winged decampment
That in their ranks will multiply!

Come take over, Fabvier, like a prince we invoke!
You who stood there alone when the loud thunder spoke,
Leaders of war-fitted armies,
Shadow of old Roman amid the newborn Greeks,
Bravest of warriors who with saber had freaked
The guts of many enemies.

From your age-long slumber, awaken already!
Guns of the French armies and wartime melody,
Bombs and cannons, spindly cymbals!
Arise horses; arise, with clamoring horseshoes,
Swords that have yet tasted what has trampled our shoes,
Handguns loaded with piercing balls!

I want a first-row glance at these fiercely combats!
See the sea of spahis with swords, handguns, and bats
On their armies wreak sheer terror.
See the way the damasks that adorn all their steeds
Dismantle their crescent, escaping at great speed!
Come on! Poet, oh what! Error!

Where are they taking me, all these bellicose bouts?
Amid elders and kids, there are my whereabouts!
What am I? Spirit of mortal.
Just like a fallen leaf from the most common birch,
Rolling down slopy brook, from bank to bank goes lurch,
So, too, from dream to dream I stall.

Always lost in some dream of air, woods, or meadows,
I'd bask for a whole day with the sounds of oboes
Or with the shuffling of dead leaves.
And at the fall of dusk, down in a dark valley,
I love a shiny lac that the heavens tally,
Not to one star ever deceive.

I love a blazing moon, glimmering just like gold,
Rising from a thick fog or that slowly unfolds,
Beaming over a somber cloud.
Or those heavy moving wagons that in the night
Roll by those sleepy farms, spreading noise, spreading fright,
Making dogs run and bark out loud.

The Heads of the Seraglio, (I and II)

I

The nightly somber dome, with shiny stars galore,
Flickered over the sea, as lustrous as before.
Istanbul, all aglow, her face with shadows veiled,
Appeared inundated, lying there in the bay
Between heaven's glitters and the water display,
Sleeping amid a starry tale.

She might as well have been, by some twilight genies,
Suspended in the air, quiet in her crannies,
Seeing her large harems, nest of dragging boredom,
Its blueish roofs liking heavenly reflection
And their golden crescents shining imitation
Of the moon quarterly stardom.

You could see the towers with angular designs,
Houses with flat domes, mosques with arrow signs,
The Moorish balconies with clover like facades,
Stained glass always hidden behind a subtle fence,
The golden palaces, and with imperial stance,
The palm trees in standing parades.

There, solid minarets with needle soaring high,
Favor ivory masts with spear spiking the sky,
You see colorful kiosks and display of lanterns,
And on the old harem that the tall walls reveal
And the tin cupolas shining with their white steel
With a blind eye can be discerned.

II

But that night, the harem was all jumping for joy.
At the sounds of the drums, over the rugs deploy',
All the sultanas danced under its sacred vault,
And like a king adorned for the rarest of feast,
Who came out, superb, to show off its A-list,
Its crowd ready with no default.

Livid, mournful looking, with well-adorned black hair,
The heads would come and top over slots here and there,
The terraces blooming of jasmine and of rose.
And like a sad consort, silently consoling,
The moon, star of the dead, over their pale shading,
Shed down its glow pale and morose.

Towering the harem, right through the main portal,
Three of them distinctly adorned the dome central.
Those heads, always battered by a black raven wing,
Seemed to have been branded by a murderous mark,
One amid the battles, one in pious remarks,
The last one befalling death sting.

They said that, but meanwhile, immobile as they were,
Ever closely watching, standing silent keepers,
The three heads suddenly spoke, and their tone of voice
Reminded of the airs of the sweetest of dreams,
Of murmur of waters entering a brook steam,
Of the breeze when the woods rejoice.

Canaris

When a conquered warship drifts about in high seas
With sails loosely dangling,
Flopping around its masts, by many bullets seized,
All torn beyond mending,

That all around, corpses piling in every part,
Anchor, tackles, and sails,
With mainmast all broken, with ropes slinging apart,
Unfastened from their nails,

That the vessel filled up with smoke and frantic noise
Goes around and around,
That people all over run with no chosen poise;
Over the floor they pound.

When at the least command no living soul takes heed,
That the sea swells and roars,
That the muted cannons drowning, like full of mead,
Bang against the decor.

That the giant vessel, through its wide-open breach,
Guzzles the sea waters,
And bleeding, as it seems, far beyond repair reach,
The whole galley clatters,

That she floats aimlessly, like a wounded carcass,
With big gap in her hull,
Like a gigantic fish with belly made of brass,
By a bigger fish mauled.

All hail to the winner! Its black anchor smashes
Against the stricken boat,
Like a strong eagle claws its prey and then slashes
In the battle its throat!

Then leans on the mainmast, as if in a tower,
With flag waving in air,
And golden reflection, sheer display of power,
That the sea judges fair.

And that's when you can see other nations display
The winner flag proudly,
And multicolored flags, in the blue sky by day,
Flop in the air loudly.

In this perfect milieu, unbridled in their pride,
They boast loud; they boast more
As if there were no end to their all-frenzied ride,
Life-and-death metaphor.

Malta brandished its cross, Venice, O you winners.
Upon its strolling sterns,
The heraldic lion roars and renders meaner
No lioness that yearns.

Naples flag in the air batters the southern skies;
Anytime it unfurls,
It's as if you can see its true nature and size
In the shape of its curls.

Spain draws flickering folds to its battering flag
Of its miserly fleet,
Léon, golden lions; Castile, of towers brags;
Navarra, its chains, beats.

Rome has its keys; Milan, the child still howling
While between the beast's teeth,
While the French naval fleet, lily flowers showing,
Contrast with coral reef.

The Turkish Istanbul, around its loathed crescent,
Displays three horses' tails.
America, now free, spreads golden stars lucent
That every state entails.

Austria's strange eagle, ready to take its flight,
Shines bright on the surface,
Threatened on either side, decides to set its sight,
The darker side to face.

Russia's eagle guarding both worlds at the same time,
Its czar, remembering,
Playing it safe, indeed, keeps four eyes on its prime,
Holding the world in string.

England, when in triumph, impresses the high seas;
Its splendid oriflamme,
And so bright was its shine that when anyone sees,
They think the sea's enflamed.

That is how the great kings, on their vessel mainmasts,
Display their coat of arms
And force the defeated to come forsake their past,
Not using any charm.

They drag within their midst these flags with sour fate
And somber destiny
And proudly they display their spoils at winner dates,
Devoid of mutiny.

To the captive vessels, forever they will teach
Their flags of victory
Just so that they can learn and turn around and preach
About their great glory.

But the good Canaris, who left a blazing trail
From his daring sailboat,
Everyone he defeats, as to warm up their sails,
Gives them flames as a coat.

Heaven's Fire I, IX and X

I

Do you see drawing by the dark and heavy cloud?
It is crimson or gray, looking mighty and proud,
Bearer of mournful frown?
At times it seems to be that the strong nightly wind,
Comes chase away the smog and blasting noise that screened
The flogging of two towns.

Was it spewed from heavens? From the sea, the mountains?
Is it of the demons, the chariot that contains
Fire from some fetid planet?
O terror! Do you see this hellish disaster,
Shooting down the dazzling, the lightning that blasters,
Just like serpents, raging, upset?

IX

Twas said that as to watch some dreaded affliction,
The prisoner firmly grasps the bars of his cage.
He could perceive Babel, guilty of same action,
Peering in wretched fright over the old-world stage.

You could hear, all throughout, this dreadful enigma,
The loudest blast filling the whole world in dismay.
Twas so deep that it shook, beyond the earth magma,
The crowd of deaf beings, recalling their doomsday.

X

The fire went raging! Not one of the condemned
Could escape the showers spreading hell upon them,
Still lifting up their hands in vain.
The ones who in embrace bade farewell to dear ones,
Frightened and terrified, wanted to know for once
Why this magma was so driven.

Against the burning rocks coming down from the sky,
Their large roof of marble, to resist, failed to try.
God always gets those who dare Him.
They prayed to silly gods, but the scolding fire
Destroyed these mute statues, ignoring the dire
Fate inflicted by the Supreme.

And so all disappeared in a black cloud of smoke,
The humans, the cities, and all that could evoke
A thought of that anathema.
Nothing stood to remind of this forsaken crowd;
Everything was wrapped up in history's dark shroud,
Ending this moral dilemma.

Nowadays, any tree, sprouting from any trench,
Breathing the deadly fumes with malodorous stench
Has its sap dry and leaves wither.
No longer they exist, these cities of the past,
And upon their ruins rises a smoking blast
That the span of time can't smother.

Vintage Parody

Dear friend, may God grant your prayers!
May hunger never shed layers
On your banquet against your will!
That never greedy misery
Imprints its claws to self-bury
Into your mantle thinning feel!

Can you, at times, my dear comrade,
Bring Bacchus into your naiad
And yourself, never so limit
To the delights ever famous
That made Curius glorious,
That Esau loved to permit!

And that through your shattered window
You never experience the blow
Of a north wind with sharpened teeth!
That in winter, while you're awake,
You never fan, in a mistake,
Your hearth ashes, causing you grief!

That your forehead, Notus pleasing,
Always the shinning armor bring
Of the water-loving beaver!
And that never your old cothurn
In the cold winter, in return,
Cause you to sink in the river!

The Legend of the Nun

Come, come you with the shiny eyes.
Come, listen to one more story.
Come nearer; together we'll size
Padilla del Flor's short glory.
She's from Alanje, where appear
Hills and bushes, growing in ton.
Children, beware, the bulls are here.
Put away any red ribbon.

Dames are plenty in Granada;
In Sevilla, just as many
Who for a sweet serenada
Would gladly change their destiny.
Many of them, bereft of fear,
At night would kiss the daring dons.
Children, beware, the bulls are here.
Put away any red ribbon.

Padilla was not of the kind,
The kind so shallow and flighty.
She never fell in such a bind;
So unique she was in beauty.
She bluntly far away would steer
From those men ready to come on.
Children, beware, the bulls are here.
Put away any red ribbon.

Never would flinch her sturdy heart,
No sweet nothings, no silly wink.
She never claimed the name sweetheart;
No loving eyes caused her to sink.
Guys are always ready to cheer.
For some ladies, it's a turn-on.
Children, beware, the bulls are here.
Put away any red ribbon.

She joined the Toledo convent,
To everyone's somber surprise,
As though ugly ones only went
And be to God a spousal prize.
For little more and you'd see tears
Shed by men every class thereon.
Children, beware, the bulls are here.
Put away any red ribbon.

She would repeat, "How sweet it is
Of this world to be far away!
What a joy! How peaceful is this
To sing your heart out and pray!
From the devil we have no fear,
For always the angels watch on."
Children, beware, the bulls are here.
Put away any red ribbon.

No longer was she in retreat
That she met with the prongs of love;
A boasting thug came took the seat
So others men had long dreamed of.
Often thugs to ladies appear
Hotter than great many a don.
Children, beware, the bulls are here.
Put away any red ribbon.

He was an ugly, rowdy boy
With a rough and strange demeanor
But became her most precious toy
She loved him when he was meaner.
The heart always is known to veer
In minefield despite the reason.
Children, beware, the bulls are here.
Put away any red ribbon.

To enter the holy cloister
And cross over the chaste hurdle,
His devilish self to hoister,
The thug smartly chose to girdle
A monk's apparel not to smear
Any doubt among any nun.
Children, beware, the bulls are here.
Put away any red ribbon.

Padilla dared, from what they say,
With the thug sent right out from hell,
Set a meeting at night to pray
Near the bust of Santa Raquel,
A time when owls brazenly jeer,
And to the bats, it's a turn-on.
Children, beware, the bulls are here.
Put away any red ribbon.

What she wanted, anathema!
Forsaking her most precious dream,
Was to settle her dilemma
On the church pews amid the dim
Candlelights and the so austere
Glance of the saints as they watch on.
Children, beware, the bulls are here.
Put away any red ribbon.

But when she went into the nave
And softly called her wretched thug,
Instead of the voice of her brave,
Of thunder she got a strong tug.
God wanted to strike with great fear
The two lovers Satan rode on.
Children, beware, the bulls are here.
Put away any red ribbon.

Nowadays, shepherds beef up tales
With mighty wrath from God above.
They tell about gigantic whales
That'd swallow some maiden betroth',
Keeping her safely for ten years
To stop her from wedding Ramon.
Children, beware, the bulls are here.
Put away any red ribbon.

When at night, the gothic abbey,
Darkening the gaping portals,
Changes everything that could be
Into objects far from festal,
At the dark hour when the mere
Set of wings ducks the horizon.
Children, beware, the bulls are here.
Put away any red ribbon.

A nun comes equipped with a lamp
As rings midnight from up a cage,
And on the wall, two shadows ramp,
Closing quickly upon the stage.
The clanging of the chains, you hear,
But closely, you can perceive none.
Children, beware, the bulls are here.
Put away any red ribbon.

In and out a gaslight shines,
Disappears under the cradle,
Then flickers but never defines
The specter behind the saddle,
And one by one, the many deer'
Shadows dance around the stallion.
Children, beware, the bulls are here.
Put away any red ribbon.

In the fire, dancing shadows,
All around, dragging their torn shrouds,
Try to alleviate their sorrow
But get lost in the thinning clouds.
You hear their footsteps drawing near
Then and throughout all the seasons.
Children, beware, the bulls are here.
Put away any red ribbon.

Now appears the fairy staircase,
Always brawling up their difference.
One, of the other, comes erase
The smallest hint of transparence.
They live just to trouble the spheres,
Shining throughout the decathlon.
Children, beware, the bulls are here.
Put away any red ribbon.

And from the tomb you hear voices,
Calling out to one another
They seem to forget the choices
Yet shout and shout with no bother,
But their calling falls in deaf ears
And swings back in sheer unison.
Children, beware, the bulls are here.
Put away any red ribbon.

And the raindrops, falling heavy,
Batter against the cold windows;
The wind blows, shaking the ivy.
You hear whistling as an echo,
And loud sighs suddenly appear,
But the thunder still carries on.
Children, beware, the bulls are here.
Put away any red ribbon.

Then a voice murmurs in the dark,
"When will all this come to an end?"
And a strong one loudly remarks,
"But eternity never ends."

And time puts on a dreary gear
Amid minutes, amid seconds.
Children, beware, the bulls are here.
Put away any red ribbon.

Hellish fires cannot be quelled,
And every night, in this tower,
A white shadow comes cast a spell
To wake up the somber power,
And together they disappear
In the fiery horizon.
Children, beware, the bulls are here.
Put away any red ribbon.

If these echoes trouble the soul
Of one traveling all alone,
That he inquires of the whole
Matter of angels liking drone,
The writings come out and smear
Every truth, thus forgetting none.
Children, beware, the bulls are here.
Put away any red ribbon.

So the story of that novice
From the bishop was required
To preserve in the state of bliss
Every maiden God acquired,
To be narrated and put fear
In all convents of Tarascon.
Children, beware, the bulls are here.
Put away any red ribbon.

Two Archers

'Twas at that mournful time of the dead of the night
That the fear of old ghosts, awakening deep fright,
Of some old drunken djinn, from some drunken orgy,
That the lone traveler, his prayer murmuring,
Ever so quickly sprints, dashing through the clearing,
Muttering trusted liturgy.

Two archers casually strolling to their hustle,
Down the somber valley, near some forlorn castle,
With tower likening, of the old Palestine,
The castles erected as tomb for ancient kings,
As per hearsay, built up by monks quickly working
While chanting formula pristine,

That the daring archers, their dinner preparing,
Lit up a bush fire in this barren setting.
They chose then to recline and rest their weary hinds
On a granite statue, tossed on the muddy ground,
Of a saint in prayer, still in a plea profound,
Determined his retort to find.

The fire bright ablaze lit up the surroundings,
The tower and the mounts, the old wooden dwelling.
The owls, all freaked out, hushed up their interlude;
The bats, frankly disturbed, zoomed into the fire,
Unable as it seemed to fly any higher,
Fanning the flames as they collude'.

The older one's humor said to the other fast,
"Do you have a cheelice?" – "Are you keeping the fast?"
Replied the younger one, and they both cracked out loud.
As a direct response, they heard a laughter fly.
The vale all deserted, they thought twas a reply
From the echo, boasting and proud.

Suddenly came a glow, floating right from the soil;
It snaked blueish furrows as if a ghost had toil'
The ground. The blasphemers, belittling it all,
Only fed more wood sticks to the candescent blaze,
Saying to each other, utterly unamazed,
"It's just a fiery recall."

But this echo (of fright everyone should shudder)
Was Satan, on the mount, cracking up much louder.
And the light reflecting from this wretched spirit
Was the make-believe glow that, in the somber night,
He spreads all around him as sample of the plight
Wreaking his deep eternal pit.

To the profane echo of their blaspheming joke,
He showed up, excited, as though he was evoke'.
And like a predator, ready to devour,
"Go ahead, have your fun. Crack all your yellow teeth.
I'll sweep up your cackle, like does a common thief
Give you one yellow and sour."

In the early morning, over a pile of soot,
A print large and all forked was left of a big foot.
The valley remained calm and quiet all day through.
But a shepherd, at night, instead of that fire,
Met that old blueish flame, burning but not higher
Than the most common chapel pew.

As soon as, on the ground, the flame started crawling,
A guffaw loud and long rose up and went lasting,
And the shepherd shuddered, all trembling of torment.
He never saw Satan, neither the dead archers
Nor could have he conceived, shaking in his bleachers,
The deep pain in their merriment.

From then on, every night, deep in the wooden mounts,
The blueish light came up, snaking the whereabouts,
The loud and cold cackles, every owl chased away,
And the old flying bats, searching places to hide,
Bumped to one another, bolting from side to side,
Totally freaking of dismay.

Nothing ever put off this dreading blueish light
Except the blessed rays of the dawn pure and bright.
And if a thunderstorm were to ring in the air,
The blasted laughter still was heard loud, was heard plain.
Then the blue light would crawl and, though hard to explain,
To join the lightning seemed to dare.

But on one blessed night, armed with his scapular,
The old granite statue rose, marble secular,
Then walked three steps toward, with blessed palm unscreened,
The dreadful blueish light, the dreading exorcist,
From his cold, stony lips quoted the old psalmist,
"May God rebuke you, wretched fiend!"

And right there it all stopped, flame, laughter, and blue light
And in the early dawn, just imagine the fright,
They found two archers dead, sitting on the statue.
They were quickly buried. The lord of the borough,
Trying to quell it all, had to pay large a dough
For masses to their soul rest, due.

If there is a lesson to draw from this story,
There's none! But rather give to God all the glory.
Could be hard to digest by the crowd nowadays,
But nonetheless, it tells of good over evil,
The well-proven power, at every known level
Then, now, and till the end of days.

Ad Majorem Dei Gloriam

They said, "We sure will be the winners and masters.
Soldiers in the tactic, priests at time of vespers,
Destroying progress, laws, virtues, rights and talents.
We'll raise up strong ramparts on these mountains of ruins
To safeguard the stances, in front like in between,
Muzzle free, owling dogs, and all biases grant.

"Yes, the scaffold is good. War is necessary.
Accept the ignorance and accept misery.
Hell awaits, with his pride, the winning magistrate.
Man gets to the angel right after the nozzle,
And our government, with force and ruse, dazzles
The father, which it gags, the son, it hebetates.

"Our ideas, hostile to the old century,
Will roll from the pulpit, like flakes on coterie,
To cool down the many hearts still indecisive,
Will freeze every needed and salutary sprout,
Then it will melt away, like the snow, with no clout,
That when they'll look for it, they never will retrieve.

"But a deep somber freeze will choke down every soul,
And we will have smothered the light they so uphold,
And if someone would say to those men of that time
Safeguard the dear freedom your fathers gained and paved!
They would laugh, all those men, exiting all their caves,
Of their lost freedom and their fathers' silent chime.

"Priests, we will write boldly on the flag shining bright:
Order and religion, wealth, family. All rights.
And if a pagan crook, Jewish or Corsican,
Would lend a hand, swearing all under the heavens,
Saber between his teeth, with torch, gory, intense,
Stealing and murdering, we would tell him, Good then!

"Winners, all fortified, well secured in strongholds,
We'll live proud and haughty, revered but won't uphold
Nor Christ nor Mahomet nor Mithra, whoever,
We'll rule as it's our goal, condemn as it's our mean.
If ever down below, our joy their ears glean,
Deep in the human heart, all fibers will quiver.

"We'll bind the very soul deep within a dark cave.
Nations, the mere essence of the people we save,
It is the monk of Spain or fellah of the Nile.
Down with the mind! Down with the law! Long live the spade!
What is it of the thought? Just a poor dog you trade.
Let's put Jean-Jacques in jail and Voltaire out of style.

"If the mind makes a fuzz, then we will smother it.
We'll go on whispering in the ears and repeat.
We will have the pontoons, Africa, the Spielberg.
The old pyres are dead. We'll bring them back to life.
Not burning human beings we'll burn books with no strife.
Instead of old Jan-Hus we'll destroy Guttenberg.

"As to the great reason that tends to condemn Rome,
Beacon that God planted inside everyone's dome,
Who guided Socrates and enlightened Jesus,
We, just like the robber who sneaks right in and crawls,
And will start, first of all, by stifling any brawl:
Tiptoeing in, we'll shut its great light around us.

"Then deep in the human soul, all dark and all somber,
Upon cold, hollow hearts we'll build the real power.
Whatever we desire, we'll get it in a hush.
Not a breath of a sound, not a shuffle of wings
Will be seen in the dark, and whatever we bring
Will be a dark tower, much darker than night brush.

"So we'll rule, for the peat is as fluid as water.
We'll be all powerful. To us none will falter.
We will own everything: might, power, happiness.
And we will fear nothing, all lawless and craven."
-"When you'll share habitat with eagles, near heaven,
I'll pull you down Myself," says the Lord, His Highness!

Sacer Esto

No, freedom! No, people, this one here cannot die!
Oh! Yes, this would have been much too simple, really,
That right after breaking the laws and certified
The time when chastity back to heavens rallied,

That right after he won this, his bloody wager,
And toppled the pitfalls, the sword, and the fire,
That after his ambush, his murders, all major,
His false oaths, so designed, God's mercy to tire,

That after he dragged down the country on its knees.
And by its feet tied up to his blasted chariot,
This disgrace would get off with death, like the many,
Like Pompey, like Cesar, by the blade! O riot!

No! he's the murderer, prowling around the fields;
He had killed with the sword, with bullets, no remorse.
He emptied the houses, yet the graveyards, he filled.
He walks his wretched way, stared down by every corpse.

Just because of this man, so transient emperor,
The son is fatherless, and the child has no hope.
The widow loudly wails and weeps, and sheer terror
Reigns around the mother who reticently mopes.

To sew his royal gowns, they color the strong thread
With the dripping red blood of his many victims.
Montmartre Boulevard provided watersheds,
And his purple mantle was tinted with blood streams.

He creates in Cayenne, Africa, in sewers,
Martyrs, deceased heroes, and convicts of today!
The cutlass red of blood, displayed to all viewers,
Letting the blood to drip, drop by drop, on his way.

And when good old treason, his livid companion,
Comes and knocks at his door, he quickly lets her in,
He kills any human, making no omission.
People, that's the reason that his life's worth saving!

Let's keep the man alive. It's fitted punishment!
Oh! If only one day he could walk by this way,
Naked, bent, shivering, like the grass, by winds bent,
Under the aversion of the world of his days!

Embraced by his past and submerged by all his crimes,
Just like a straitjacket, ruffled up by old prongs,
Searching for hidden sites, forests, and dens with slime,
Pale, horrible, flurry, with wolves, where he belongs.

In some loathsome slammer, with the cling of his chains,
Forever on his own and entertaining rocks,
Sensing all around him silence and sheer disdain,
No living soul around just shadows behind locks.

Getting old, rejected by death, found unworthy,
Trembling in the dark night, dreadful at the blue sky…
People, stand back! This man you see walking loathly:
Make way for Cain. I say, let God, his snares, untie.

The Poet to Himself in 1848

You should not chase after power but do instead
Your work away from it, mind by the Spirit led.
Facing up temptation, pull far away, simply.
To the wavering thoughts, show your love steadily.
Admired by a crowd and by others despised,
You must be their shepherd or priest with no disguise.
When you see citizens angered from misery,
Daughters of the same town, sons of the same country,

Clash, and points the bleak sight of the barricade stand,
This depressing display seen in every street band
Brings about striking prongs, heart-wrenching dejection,
You must alone stand out, unarmed in objection,
For in this wretched war, infamous and loathsome,
Offer up your bare chest; spill your soul, and then some.
Beg, pray, and supplicate to the weak and the strong.
Smile to the machine guns; to the dead, cry a song,

Then go back peacefully to your den retire,
And there defend your cause, with all your strength dire,
Amid the assembly. The ones unfortunate,
Save from the guillotine; the weak ones, insulate.
The order and the peace that shake one stubborn group,
Misleading the soldiers stifling the growing coup,
The poor man of the street jailed for crying hunger,
For trampling of the laws, loss of freedom, angered.

In these most dreadful days of misery, console.
Then the divine face who laments under the toll
And waits for the right time, troubled and weighed down,
Will admonish and lead while pondering your frown.

And on That Night

Three friends were there with him. Twas at the Elysée.
The bright light shining in from outside you could see,
Keeping track of the time, the clock needles moving.
He was lost in his thoughts, planning while daydreaming
To mix Bonaparte's name to exploits in cartouche;
He felt nearing the trap of that old bag of douche.

Facing the hearth, his foot vaguely kicking the brand,
This is then that he said that man on treason stand,
"Tonight I will unveil all my secret projects.
The Saint-Barthelemy's are possible as yet.
Paris sleeps, and just like under Charles de Valois,
You'll put in a big bag all the laws, with no noise,

And then over the bridge, toss them all in the Seine."
O ruffians! You bastards of proceeds much obscene,
Fruits of sinful coitus of scheme and wretched fate!
Just by thinking of you, my rhymes flow all irate!
And my heart deep inside thunders within my chest
Just like a swinging oak deep within the forest!

As they were exiting, all three from the Bancal's
Morny, Maupas, the Greek, Saint-Arnaud, the jackal,
Seeing this group walk by, all skewed and taciturn,
With Paris bells tolling with tone grave and nocturne,
Trying hard to mimic the dread of a tocsin,
The July cobblestone was yelling, "Assassin!"

Every bloody scepter from those old carnages,
Awakened, was pointing at these personages.
The Marseillaise, strong hymn, archangel of anthem,
Was subtly exhorting, "Rise up! To all of them!
Paris still in slumber! And soon in all the squares,
On the docks, the soldiers, with usual docile stare,

And janissaries led by Reybell and Sauboul,
Paid like in Byzantium, drunk like in Istanbul,
Those of Dulac and those of Korte and Espinasse,
Loaded with cartridges and breathing pure menace,
Came down in great number of scrolling regiments,
Steaming down every street, parading the pavements,

They hushed come like tigers from faraway jungles,
Crawling on their stomach, claws ready to strangle.
And in that gloomy night, Paris remained dormant,
Like a sleeping eagle in dark entanglement.
The chiefs smoked their cigars, scanning the shades of dawn.
O Cossacks! Thieves! Chauffeurs! Teamsters! Bulgarians! Pawns!

O general robbers! Oh, prison, take them all!
Longtime-ago judges, for much lesser downfalls,
Had the Voisin burned up and Desrues sternly flogged!
Displaying down the streets the vile posters they hugged
And the recreant plot of those daring tricksters,
And morning came. Darkness, which favors all gangsters,

Flew away still dragging its veil in great hurry,
Disrobing the bright sky of stars in its fury,
And the many glitters that shimmer in the night.
Like the golden sequins that would take in her flight,
A girl, after the act performed with so many,
Would rush to put her clothe once she gets her money.

The Voyage

The horse rings its harness. Long ago, all ready,
The pavement in reply echoes its melody.
It's time for departure. Chase away the concerns
Stifling your gentle heart. I know how much you care.
The wagon pulls away, leaving you on this square.
Sadly, your tears now I discern.

Remain there and follow with eyes clouded by tears.
Let out drop by drop this long-expected fear
To see me leave your side, to tear us all apart.
Already we belong to some different sphere;
Already I don't see your face I held so near,
And ever far from you will beat my bleeding heart!

Not even the least sound, not a fleeting shadow,
Deep inside within me all is bleak and hollow.
And every mile I run further seals the cold tomb
Where I now will endure raw and distressing fright,
The dread of your absence, the anguish and the plight.
My soul to this nightmare succumbs.

What will become of me and my thoughts running wild?
What will I tell my soul missing your arms so mild
And your embrace so warm and the touch of your hands?
I drown in bitter waves while my buoy's afar.
I tiptoe in darkness without my guiding star.
What will become of me in this faraway land?

Vaguely, as in a dream, my eyes follow the scene.
Everything comes and goes, repulsive, quite obscene.
The offered paysage seems so bleak and austere;
Nature in early spring never looked so barren
As though, of its seasons, it would have lost the reins
And the sun ran away in fear.

Trees, houses, and mountains, nothing really matters;
The overcast heavens entomb my gray matter
And tint my universe of a dull, sullied look.
Why will I see beauty that with you I can't share,
And sunshine if to it, your eyes I can't compare?
My willow languishes far away from your brook.

From now on, so sadly, there will be days ahead
Where, next to my lost soul, I will not hear you tread.
I will see the sun rise yet miss its blessed glow.
There will be sunny days that will miss your brown eyes,
And the sunsets will thwart the show of crimson skies,
Sad days to sad days will follow.

But I have to man up; have to, against these odds,
Tell you words of comfort to warm your heart a tad.
Tell you not to worry, that soon it'll be over,
That far away from you, I lament and wither;
And create funny jokes to make your heart lighter
While my universe pines under gloomy cover.

What are you doing now? How was your day at work?
Or, as often the case, are you trying to perk
One of your patients up from some daunting outcome?
Life is full of surprise. Often what you hold near,
Without any warning, away from you may steer,
Leaving you stranded and lonesome.

And deep within yourself, you wonder where he is;
Has he already passed the county of "Sea Breeze?"
Is he thinking of me, lost in the scenery?
Has he yet forgotten the ones he left behind?
Has he, in an attempt, his peace of mind to find,
Lost himself in that sight fairy?

But this good old patient -behold- now therapist,
Reminds you of praying one should never desist,
That always, in all things, whenever needs arise,
The pilgrim on this earth should seek help from above.
"Ask and you shall receive," says the Master of Love,
Ask for some solace for your eyes.

For before you know it, he will be by your side.
The dune never desists when awaiting the tide.
I take it you breathe in whatever he exhales,
That hand in hand, your souls have been on this journey.
But love grows much fonder when away for many,
Whereas much exposure often renders it stale.

So there, my better half, there your loved one remains,
On this forlorn voyage, among tress, among plains.
But never, not a speck, has of your sweet visage
He ever lost trace of and of your eyes the glow.
Hopefully, next to you, by a quick tomorrow,
He'll return back to your sweet cage.

Thanksgiving

You so ever safely led me back to the shore;
I grew back in wisdom, in peace, and in candor,
Dear Lord, I give You thanks! Unlike ever before,
You rekindled my lamp and restored its splendor.

Caught up in the tempest, eaglet devoid of wings,
Falling to its demise, down to the smallest shrub,
Gentle cub that I was, unaware of the swing
Startled by the winds that against my cradle rub.

Oh! From my very dawn, life for me was a drag
Although from the heavens, I ever got a break,
It was never allowed that with my empty bag,
I would be, so early, befallen with heartache.

My teenage years were full of glittering fables,
Of glorious future, of love and swollen pride,
But when feverishly for them I went grabble,
One after the other, away from me they'd slide.

So away from the cloud, I chose to retire,
Much at peace with my pain but bereft of remorse.
I carried my sorrow, facing the satire,
Such orphan that I was, lost in life's dreaded course.

With hopes ever secured, I went into this maze,
Daring so brazenly my hardship to affront.
That's when in me geysered, all-ready and ablaze,
Deep from my lonesome mind, ideas with words in front.

`And like John in Pathmos, my mind went on a spree;
All was given to me, imbedded in this fright.
And the gloomy tincture of my mind wild and free
Invaded all my lines, blurring my sobbing sight.

Slowly and yet surely my gaiety dimmed away,
O Lord, as it seemed then, You had forsaken me.
I carried my burden but never once displayed
Anger toward Your sky or uttered blasphemy.

I write this truthfully so that the world may read
That I remained faithful in the midst of sorrow.
Give all glory to God, whose flock He always leads
From the greenest pasture to clearest water flow!

Then the Lord said to me, "Go, my son, take my yoke,
For in adversity, you were ever faithful.
Since in your darkest hour my name you still evoke',
Girdle the white garments among all the joyful."

No more will I offer, from my somber solace,
The ever-shining torch of eternal glory,
From the flowing spirit's ingenious embrace
With bright and soaring rays telling the tomb story.

Nowadays, over me, a kind angel hovers;
An orphan to her eyes, appears a precious pearl.
Of my once gloomy soul, she is the sole lover;
And breathing the same air, we go around the world.

For You ever safely led my boat back to shore,
I flourished in wisdom, in peace, and in candor.
Dear Lord, to You all praise! For like never before,
You rekindled my lamp and restored its splendor.

The Name

Purest lily essence, soft glow of aureole,
The last murmur heard of the day,
Lament of a dear friend that saddens and consoles,
The illusive farewell of the hour that tolls,
The tender sound of love display,

The most beautiful bow drawn in the midst of haze
As a thunderous kiss to a triumphant sun,
And the sudden timbre calling you out of daze,
Your most treasured first love's ingenious first praise.
Fond wishes from your endeared nun.

The distant chorus ring, the early dawn murmur
That exhaled the famous Memnon,
The whisper of a sound fading to the azure,
Every thought you harbor to peace of mind, assure,
Of this sweet name equals in none!

Whisper it as softly as a faithful prayer,
But let it ring out loud in every blessed hymn!
Let its light softly glow, making temples gayer!
That it'd be repeated, like securing layer,
In the temple as blessed theme.

Dear friends, let us before, with words sharp and ablaze,
My muse, losing her train of thought,
Dares to all other names, lost in this worldly maze,
Mix this most revered name she'd rather not rephrase
But keep deep inside of her vault;

We'll have to make the ring of these most treasured hymns
Like those every faithful intones on bended knees,
That at their solemn sounds the congregation seems
To see hosts of angel hover in deep esteem,
Singing along in harmony.

Paysage

Once upon a long time, my muse said to me, "Come;
"Come and see the wonders I have for you in store.
Everything I possess, as ambit of kingdom,
Be it bright metaphors or reverenced wisdom,
Ready to be birthed in your core!

"But you must, of yourself, treasure the company,
Away from the gossip, away from what is vile.
Always when surrounded by the vibes of many,
What should flow into you, of goodness, if any,
May lose its form, may lose its style!

"Choose a humble setting and make it your abode.
Go hide this blessed light under some safe bushel.
There in a peaceful trance, you will gently implode,
And free of envious minds, you will receive the code
That your drought of soul will dispel!

"One will never fathom the purview of the soul.
Always submerge your mind in harmonious ponds.
Delight your fancy heart, allow it to extol
And reach highest mountains to the heavens' threshold,
Where you and I can safely bond!

"Make it a suited vale, your place of convergence,
So that amid the shrubs and assorted flowers,
You may guess the passing, in their sheer elegance,
Of angels frolicking in their celestial dance
Around some medieval tower

"That hangs over the pond from an old mountain side
And whose trail, deep winding, leads the eyes to nowhere.
Some cozy wood fire at night whose smoke would hide
The stars flickering sight and up to the moon glide,
        With insects buzzing here and there.

"That gliding graciously, two waves in sweet fury
Come to your soul display their lovely grade of foam
And a low passing cloud unveil the true fairy,
The magical vigor driving each and every
        Wave that deep within the lac roams.

"That in your mental stroll on your favorite island,
With cool and shady shore of the greenest foliage,
The soothing elation caused by this blissful land
Gets you to decipher, lying upon the sand,
        The winds and flowing wave verbiage.

"That gleeful, you wake up with a festive chorus,
Spreading in the warm air their choice of tender themes
Where the subtle notion of the so frivolous
Of childhood escapades brings from your subconscious
        The hopes and love; core of your dreams.

"That some humble owner, with gentle attitude,
Would've lorded this land with justice and with grace,
That recalling his name and gracious habitude,
The elders all around would say with certitude
How sweet is living in this place.

"Far away from the world is where we'll ever meet,
And I'll pour within you the fondest of motives
That to you, wide open, notions of the Spirit,
Well engraved on your mind, will spring you on your feet
And broadly stir all relatives!"

And so it was uttered, straight, O my gracious muse!
Although circles around, against my fleeting will,
The sound so perturbing that I cannot diffuse
Of gentle folks galore, of living so enthused,
And the so diverse roles they fill.

In order to complete what I came to fulfill,
From heaven was dispatched a warm and cheerful guide.
I breathe my very best when my spirit she fills.
With trips to distant stars, she silently instills
The bliss that deep in me resides.

One More Time

To you, and only you, once again, right out loud,
To you, my loving theme, to you, my sweet love song.
Who else on this green earth could open up the shroud
Where I lie, atoning for all that I've done wrong?

Over my darkest nights, let your guiding light glow
And let your face kindle my hearth when I slumber.
You alone hold my hand in my everyday flow,
Bringing me heaven's treats in impressive number.

Subtly, day after day, you bestow your goodness,
Hovering on my soul, ensuring my safeguard.
When you barge on my mind, I perceive your finesse,
Which gives me strength to stand what comes to my regard.

Aren't you in demand to a much worthy bunch?
Aren't you here spoiling an undeserving soul?
Precious jewel of my case, my most spirited punch,
You reveal to my soul the God I should extol.

When you set your brown eyes on my world small and bleak
And gently come and brush my wrought-up attention,
The thrill deep within me brings me up to the peak,
Where I can hear angels in blissful rendition.

When with your tender touch you came soothe all my ills
I knew then, for certain, I'd found my pot of gold;
And like the wise brethren who discerned a good deal,
To safeguard it, quickly all that I had I sold.

And I even worship the ground you tread upon,
Like the sweetest mama, well-endowed of wisdom,
Like a gentle sibling always there to lean on,
Like the only daughter you thought would never come.

Alas! I love you so that the sound of your name
Brings tears into my eyes and a knot in my throat.
And in this icy land, my heart and soul you tamed,
Pine all day and all night. So this to you I wrote.

O Lord, make that one day, one of these autumn eves,
Guided by Your Spirit, she makes her way to me.
Until this blessed day, with heart set on my sleeve,
I will pray that her eyes will never be gloomy.

Blessed Perseverance

The traveler lounges under the still shadow;
In the midst of this vale, all alone, he daydreams:
Here a cheerful bird chase, here a dancing willow
And the brook shouting muffled screams.

But nature with its laws, in many instances,
Brings to a gentle soul its share of grave burden.
Of a narrow escape, what are the fat chances
That he dies early in its den.

Here sitting in this vale, he longs for such a break,
Traveling yet so far, lacking yet what it'd take
To dismantle his miseries.
And down his weary sight only looms the faint hope
Through all the passive clouds of his arising slope
With his tomorrow's mysteries.

Gloomy and dejected, on the road straight ahead,
Nothing of his fancy can tickle the meek shed.
He craves a kindred soul for this dreary journey
But in vain, for alas, on this rotating sphere,
No one will come efface the look bleak and austere
That chases away so many.

He long gave up the fight, and the look of his stance
Favors the dark cypress, never given a chance,
In this forlorn valley. It stands tall and erect,
And never has it been, to lighten its figure
And revamp its gloomy tenure,
That a devoted vine its trunk would come prospect.

So before he resumes his long dreary travel,
After a short respite and mental escapade,
The lonely traveler, leaving the soothing shade,
Drags the hefty silence, helpless to unravel
His solitude that would not fade.

Trees, ponds, growing bushes from one another stray
Yet so serene in all your ways.
Come all and lend a hand to this young fellow's plight!
Gentle brooks; come awash with your cool flowing streams
His ever-weary feet from the mire and the themes
Of the city's numerous sights.

Under your soothing shades, grant that he comes recline
And, in sweet somnolence, his state of being refines!
And the lovely maiden, queen of his mind caper,
Who comes in every time to offer sweet solace
With her angelic voice and in tender embrace,
His gloomy heartache she'll taper.

Nothing can bind his soul, soaring high to its bliss,
To fall in unison with treasured souvenirs.
Nothing else in this life can preclude him to miss
What he once knew and what, day after day, he nears.

When will I see your face? Tell me, when will you bless,
O star with warmth aglow, O beacon of my night,
With your sweet soul, my den meekness
To cast away this dull and dreary sadness plight?

He'll never reach the shore of this isle of his dreams
Despite the deep longing of his soul in distress.
But rather he relies, as foolish as it seems,
On the goodness of He who hears the silent screams
Of those yearning for a mistress.

But O goodness! Behold! There she comes from afar!
Farewell to you, cradling streamlets!
Farewell I bid to you, sweetest vale that you are.
Farewell, bosket, venting outlet!

Blessed be the lonely who, with nature surround,
His soul's deepest illness he can just ventilate.
Since his relief cannot be found,
He trusts heavens for his clean slate.

My Soul

Proud of my provenance, I will shun earthly treats,
Remain ever humble, fondling my solitude.
I will only treasure, searching for comfort seats,
The throne or the tomb plenitude.
To all the glittering of this forsaken town,
I chose to carry not a frown,
Thus expresses the lonely soul.
I will be the focus of my gyrating sphere,
Always lull and cradle my world stark and severe,
Striving daily to remain whole.

You're forever summoned to carry on your back
The humane condition known as sorrow and pain.
Deep-rooted in the world, everyone has no lack
Of this eternal daunting stain.
To the Source of your light who sustains existence,
In all things give loud reverence.
Pray that my senses He subdues.
Over all aspects of my life, may His Spirit ever preside,
That ever subtly, night and day, in it He chooses to abide,
Preserving safely its virtues.

Since you are the true sap flowing within my lines,
Sweetest of essences, resonate in their flow.
Come in the dead of night, inspiration divine,
Be the strong bow for my arrow.
Spread over your mantle, lover of God above,
Whisper to me of His sweet love

That daily waters down the earth.
Pour deep within my heart the sweet consolation
That the spirit in you reveals to the nations
Through angels in celestial mirth.

Were you there around the time
God took pride in Creation,
Way before the crawling slime
Delivered devastation?
Did you witness at first glance
Eve entering her first dance,
At the time when paradise,
Adoring God's true brilliance
Would stand in humble audience,
Running yet at its full size?

Did you witness the downpour
From the Source of all beings,
Spreading stars from heaven's pores
For celestial glittering,
When in all heavenly bliss,
God filled up the great abyss,
His true chef d'oeuvre observing,
Him, the source of every life,
Him, solver of every strife,
Giver of every good thing?

When God drew the curtain, over time in cascade,
To reveal His big plan to angel eyes in spades,
Did you notice the frown that shook the head of hosts?
Or the startled virgin, so young and meek at heart,
Did you see Gabriel voicing to her his toast?
There, God, in His goodness, offered a brand-new start
To all His creation, all through His Holy Ghost.

Did you peep down below, over the deep abyss,
To take load of the fear and permanent jaundice
That befalls followers of the celestial foe,
Where eternal torment, like unending birth pangs,
Puts a deadly choke hold on the soul in sorrow
And crime, in its despair, continuously bangs
Its head, but every time, wrenching remorse echoes?

Show me the Almighty splitting the night from day,
Spreading time on its course, giving the sun its rays,
When with just one finger He drew the horizon
And counted to the sea its great number of drops.
When from Mary the Godchild popped,
Was it then that music got its diapason?

The spirit deep within the box case of your walls
Fuels your every voyage of which you're so enthrall'.
Even the forbidden, the land of golden dreams,
From which man was casted for all eternity,
Is found in your vicinity.
There you feed my forehead with your heavenly themes.

But take heed, O my soul, to safeguard your merits,
For the enemy roams, never once needing sleep.
The many clever traps set to make you culprit
Are ever inserted in your sought-after treats.
So be vigilant on your trips.

Be mindful of the lure of those nowadays pearls,
For to them I prefer a love chaste and candid.
If ever you rather play all over the world,
Then be it. But you'll be on your own in this swirl.
So don't go play the intrepid.

When caught in the mind games of the senseless affairs,
The ever-fickle heart responds as you predict.
Mine is not born this way and would not take an air
Knowing well it's risking an upcoming despair.
Never engineer a conflict.

In the high court, they'll say, screening your intentions,
That you failed to uphold the law of this here land.
And in just conclusion, after the inspection,
You'll be asked, rightfully, a show of contrition,
The kind you may never attend.

Therefore, remain astute, avoiding these craters.
They may not be abyss but hide their traps the same.
Better safe than sorry, and in the hereafter,
Much lesser demerits will show in your chapter
Or be posted next to your name.

Do as to, returning to face the mighty Judge,
A lesser load of dust renders you more limpid.
Everything is counted; even the slightest grudge
Will make you be sent back and return once you purge,
And you'll stand there sad and livid.

Woe to the living soul, who traverses God's land,
Shunning a clear knowledge of the Spirit at hand.
Living dust that ignores the source of the body.
He remains well ensnared and thus ever devoid
Of light. For always he's annoyed
By the least of refrain of divine melody.

Sweet Devotion

We give You thanks, O Lord, for safeguarding Your flock!
You give us life, which is heavens' most precious gift.
Always, blessed Savior, to Your table we flock
To gain solace by You bequeathed.
There, freed from this old world and its so many snares,
We live Your life all well aware
That at the end we'll see Your face.
So we bathe in Your Word, carrying all burden,
Putting all trust in You, shunning what You disdain,
Our old failures so to efface.

Woe to whosoever upon this world who trod
Then died meaninglessly, failing to leave behind
Some light upon a shelf or some seed in a pod
So that a brother his way finds.
Forsaken are the ones who ever curse laden,
With hearts so willingly harden,
Perish over their century
But failed, to the whole world, to leave wreaths of roses
But instead perpetrate what heaven opposes,
Show of spiritual penury.

Whenever in His wrath, the good Lord shows His might,
Upon the blighted group He allows disasters,
Which, in their destruction, cause such a widespread fright
That is felt long time thereafter.
Some fabricated strong virus, with appetite for lung tissues,
In their midst was wily issued.

It made its rounds so stealthily
And, on its path unknown to all and to many,
Grabbed the throats of Mary, Dick, Candy, or Lenny,
Destroying lives so woefully.

In alarming numbers, people therefore succumbed;
Nature lost its jewels like and sadly rang its knell.
Body bags amounted, and families entombed
Dear ones this dreaded curse befell.
The virus silently extinguishes the lives
By destroying their breathing drives
Feasting on cells to reproduce.
These replicas flourish in such a great number
That you're forced to cremate in fire bright amber
From fear to contagion induce.

When in the ancient Rome, in the arena, caged,
Were thrown to the wild beasts the captives they avowed,
Romans complacently witnessed bloody carnage,
Then pleasing to the cheering crowd.
Just so, many nations, all fearing and trembling,
Behind closed doors went on mumbling
To engineer the germ defeat.
They acted rapidly, much too fast as it seemed,
To come up with a cure that to the world was deemed
To put nations back on their feet.

Turfs spared were very few; the whole globe was bleeding.
There was not a safe port willing to dock a float.
And wherever you were, you could see how fleeting
Was what over which we so gloat.

And fingers were pointed; many culprits were named.
Finally, no one was to blame.
One thing remained that was certain;
No one would go to sleep not fearing next-day news.
The great many a life on which this dark foe chews
Witnessed the fall of their curtain.

And around every hearth, with warmth and peace aglow,
Every given mother treasures the life she tends.
Unaware or rather just blocking the echo
Of ambulance persistent trends.
Life as we long knew it has come to a standstill.
Of fright, the news feed us our fill.
The streets remain silent and bare,
Where the first responders can freely go their way,
Haggard and taciturn, taking back to their hay
This taste of end of time they share.

But every now and then surge a few zealous souls
Who, in the midst of it, offer more than their parts.
They stand unaffected by the daunting death toll,
Wearing upon their sleeves their heart.
You see them night and day working relentlessly,
Braving it all so fearlessly.
They seem to brazenly, as often angels do,
Heed a higher calling guiding their every move.
They go from bed to bed, attempting just to prove
That God fights our battles too.

Therefore, to those godsent, those bona fide heroes,
Who jump in the fire with no hesitation,
Who forsake their own health to relief the sorrow
Of the ones deemed to perdition,
Let us offer our prayers with much-needed support
And the kudos of any sort.
Also commend their sacrifice,
Exhort every effort to which they feel compelled
And correct, so to speak, whatever they misspelled
And offer them help once or twice.

And all over the floors, their names are being praised;
People of every tongue toward them stretch their hands,
All astounded to see so much love set ablaze.
As for us, human beings, it stands.
Just a few words from them can their worries palliate.
For facing the weight of their fate.
The least kindness comes deep to quench
The soul all dejected, which falls under a spell,
Like Satan dumfounded seeing the Lord in hell
To pull souls from his sordid trench.

They relentlessly try, way beyond their purview,
To save the least of those that lie under their care.
The ongoing battle saves the lives of a few;
Still, they do more of their fair share.
Technology tumbles, but their prayers sustain,
So peaceful solace they obtain.

Thus, heaven blesses their effort
To lead safely to shore, ready to cross over
The deeply fretting soul upon whom death hovers.
They remain their final escort.

So to the daring bunch, the ones nothing can touch,
To you who daily spring to affront the unknown,
I salute your calling, and I envy you much.
Angels in disguise well enthroned.
Although I see your names well written in His book,
I'd never muster what it took
To stand and caringly attend,
Despite knowing so well the nature of the strand,
To so many. Although my coward heart it rends;
Really, I will never pretend.

Scenes of altruism don't play upon my stage;
Despite my deep concern, I remain hesitant.
Be it a stealthy germ or exchange of hostage,
To die I remain reluctant.
It is only reserved for the not so many
Who shimmer along this journey.
Just like Peter at the cockcrow,
I'll shy away under a directed fire
And regret thereafter not having scored higher.
This is only at angels' throw.

The Almighty

All glory be to God who shines through Creation!
In the palm of His hand basks the whole universe.
He set eternity with its slotted notion,
And for infinity, boundaries He reverse'.

To wretched entropy He breathed its unity.
At the sound of His voice, the world was entity.
One by one, the nations rolled down from His phalanx,
And He measured the days. To places, He gave sights
And to centuries gave more might.
Over generations, bestowed wisdom and ranks.

In all the universe roams His blessed wisdom.
To the fleeting comet He dictates the right speed.
With one blow of His breath, hurricanes to become,
And the nights and the days to His limits, agreed.

See volcanos erupt over the raging sea
And majestic mountains bow like flowing waters.
And of the underworld, ignoring His mercy,
He casts all the demons to fiery quarters.

Lord, the whole creation flows under Your strong will,
And every living thing, of Your life is instilled!
You spread over the earth the adequate degrees.
You protect the meek ones from the greed of the haves,
And You set Your justice to plead on their behalf,
Enforcing subtly Your decrees.

Human can only thrive, led by His strong spirit.
Just a speck of His mind and he turns into dust.
In their heart He bestows, based upon their merits,
Sadness to the guilty and His bliss to the just.

The blessed hosannas ring out in His heaven,
Intoned by the choirs of blissful cherubim.
The grateful universe echoes and it's driven
Down to the underworld, where His light does not beam.

So from host of angels, the galaxies, the saints,
And all the blessed souls, the Glorias are sent.
O God ever present and ever merciful,
You created human, so weak and so mortal,
And tolerates his many falls,
Knowing that without You, he's lost and pitiful!

All glory to our Lord who shines through Creation!
In the palm of His hand basks the whole universe.
He set eternity with its slotted notion,
And for infinity, boundaries, He reverse'.

World History

As history repeats its ever-daunting self
And offers but refrains from her numerous shelves,
Bringing such an array of déjà vu problems,
My poor brain remains caught within the web of time,
Shuffling all its glories, its conquests, and its crimes
And how the book was shut on them.

I behold this great book but would not dare open
Any of its chapters riddled of joy and pain.
As it's often revealed, history teaches well,
And the ever daring who ignore their lessons
Fall in the luring traps of deceits and treasons,
And their fates all scholars can tell.

Hence, I remain silent and quietly observe,
For these themes, as always, to keen ears will be served.
And I will not reveal but won't by any means
Not with a grieving dirge or by surging shout,
Whatever the concerns are really all about
Refute again what they demean.

For when I peer over the deep reeking abyss
Of the widespread violence committed in our midst,
I hear within my soul, saddened down to the core,
The summon to recall to the ones in my reach
The true meaning of life. But I'm afraid I preach
On this theme encore and encore.

To every blasting mouth, pair of ears ought to heed,
For thus will be planted, one never knows, what seed.
For we are the many, and we carry the crown.
Seed of love, seed of faith, seed of knowledge and light,
Seed that often opens some other point of sight,
Seed of Spirit who rids all frowns.

For once he feels compelled, devoid of interests,
Those of financial greed or of ego contests.
Over the sea of souls let him spread the good seed.
There let him set ablaze and remind the many
That they are not alone on this dreary journey.
God, through prayers, their spirits, feeds.

The Solitary Man

Oh! So insidiously let him go his journey,
Lonesome and all downcast, rejected by many,
Facing up his own miseries.
Away from him depart, so desolate and stark,
Let him flourish alone, all branded by the mark
That begets all his reveries.

Subtle loads on his chest, although heavy as lead,
Weigh down on his spirit and still lead it with stead
Where suffering has its reward.
Time for him flies so fast but throughout the seasons
Resounds loud yet hollow at unmeasurable sones
His fame you cannot disregard.

Often deep in the night, alone without a prayer,
He suffers his failures, missing the much gayer
Springtime that long ago he knew.
But under the heavens where the blessed mantle
Steadily still secures what pain could dismantle,
Everything good is left to brew.

Lost in the daunting maze of this young century,
He tolerates his share of the dark knight's fury
And patiently suffers his drought.
And what heaven offers; friends, music, and talent,
All the invisible ever prompt and gallant,
At times fail to erase his pout.

Lost in deserted nights, he often cradles dreams
Where life would offer him islands of peaceful themes
As promise of needed solace.
And ever silently he'd spring to go secure
This rare pearl of wisdom that surely does assure
That heavens never lost his trace.

But in the arena where we all strive to live,
The thoughts we wear so bare one by one go through sieve,
Perturbing the flow of mischief,
For human nature drowns all in petty gossip.
Every uttered warning, selectively they sip,
Not to offend their dreaded chief.

Open the heavy gate and give him an escape
Far away from the crowd breathing too close his nape.
Give him this much-needed freedom.
What are petty visions, next to his realm, compared?
When all about your world is so loud yet so bare,
Designed to drown souls in boredom.

All alone in the midst of his glowing shadows,
When hand in hand he goes fetching the sweet echo
Trickling down from his treasured source,
There, exchanging softly his torment for rare pearls,
He peeps at the glory of the maker of worlds,
Eavesdropping on angel discourse.

The many sheep he counts turned into glowing spheres
Where glorious azures clash with the so austere
Tone of his niche with single bed.
And in the dark, he basks on the divine convoy
Of the beatified ever perpetual joy,
Adoring the mighty Godhead.

The glow of his pupils shimmers so to unveil
The nature of the touch created to prevail
Upon his humble soul purview.
For often -Oh glory! He is summoned swiftly
To come and replenish ever so rapidly
His soul from its fleeting curfew.

Cast away as he stands from the so numerous,
The so many brethren bedazzled and curious
By this talent subtly bequeathed
That now opens the doors of heavenly treasures
And consoles the humble in his simple leisure
With heavenly peace as a gift.

And as in a sudden, one day of sweet delight,
He springs out preaching, ignoring his own fright,
The truths the world deconditioned.
Ever feverishly attempting to disarm
The fabricated norms purposely set to arm
Nature's most precious foundation.

Right then he is given, as though so much ablaze,
Words straight from the furnace fully able to tase
The looming crowd blind and adrift.
And the phrases are sharp, cold as frigid water,
Waking even the dead caught in the hereafter,
Where God alone can make a rift.

Heartfelt Prayer

Now that Flushing, New York, with its overcast dome,
Its ever-busy streets, loaded buses and cars,
Its cold and snowy days, no more is called my home,
I can grasp what nature offers to me so far.

Now that all that I lost is forever made clear,
Duped, coerced, and mislead,
Now that I realized the treasure held so dear
By the void left instead,

Now that on this seashore, so warm and so friendly,
All touched by the eerie crimson evening display,
I can finally scope and perceive vividly
The trickery performed, sheer cause of my dismay,

Now that nothing hinders the flow of souvenirs,
Of missing her brown eyes,
Now that, O my dear Lord, who remains always near
To those many despise,

Now that all that I see of goodness, warmth and sun,
Loudly seem to confess Your deep love for Your brood,
The tears that now I shed atone, sine qua non
For having so bluntly disregarded the good

That You bestow on us, proof of Your loving care.
Your wisdom surpasses,
And though Your ways are just, no one should ever dare
Waste Your given graces.

Therefore beloved Father, You handed me a rose,
And in my troubled mind, I left her all alone.
Now every ounce of tears she sheds in her repose
Will be taken to me for my soul to atone.

You know, blessed Father, how precious are the tears
Shed by Your innocents.
Never an instant do You ever fail to hear
Their pleas when they are sent.

You see deep in the hearts every hidden motive;
You see the contrition that ravages the soul.
You see, and it's for us a blessed incentive
To hope for Your goodness to again make us whole.

For the angels summoned to evolve among us,
Not all have the same clout.
We only recognize the size of their genius
When they leave with sad pout.

We so poorly perceive only one side of facts.
The true meaning exists safely in Your domain.
Lovingly You take us along the chosen track
Although to heed Your voice, so stubborn we remain.

My uttered contrition and sought-for forgiveness
To Your mercy, appeal.
Send her again my way so that through Your goodness
My embrace she could feel.

Clearwater-Bound

My child, allow the sun to burn
My baldhead and mature dimples.
Let the seasons come and take turn
To bring you your father's cables.

The news will come just to reveal,
My blessed child, how is laden
Your father from all that he still
Misses so every now and then.

With teary eyes, you want to know
The reasons of my departure.
I could tell you, but such a show
Is not fit to your young stature.

What the Lord gives is too precious
For His children to mishandle.
Although He's never furious,
His justice every soul fondles.

He summoned so to make amend,
In exile, I go mend my soul.
Solitude will suffice to rend
My heart, so His name I extol.

So like the birds, I am southbound,
Hoping to mend my failing heart.
I will go where the sea resounds.
I will go where the sun departs.

Keep deep within your tender core
The cold nights and each Sunday mass.
So that we share the same decor
Chewing on souvenirs amass'.

I am bound for this sunny shore
Where suffering seems much lighter.
I never went that road before,
But know your dad is a fighter.

I pray my God your soul to keep;
He knows us so, so much better.
I will take as many a trip
As allowed here from Clearwater.

He took the blow, keeping all in,
Not even once mumbles a sound.
His life forever had caved in
Now that his father was southbound.

Way Down

I can honestly say, and it's without a doubt,
That in the midst of all the troubles I incur,
Facing the lack of drive that steadily recurs
And the given support devoid of any clout,

Now that nature rebirth, once so dear to my sight,
Is not worth any pence, rather highlights my drought.
Now that I barely taste, lost in perpetual pout,
The love heaven bestows on whom is found delight.

This inner war I waged since I can remember
Looks as senseless and bleak, with no aim at its end.
Now that all deflated, I no longer pretend
To be what I once sought, feeling so dismembered.

Now that away from all that made so meaningful
The life I lived thus far, root of my tomorrow,
That the golden sunrays penetrate just to show
The barren of my world, grievous and pitiful.

I have to draw curtain and renounce all efforts
That well upon this earth kept me breathing thenceforth.
The thoughts of other dawn or any life henceforth
Torment my troubled soul with darts of any sort.

For over and over upon this once-green earth,
I swotted painfully to overcome my miss.
But deeper and deeper I fall in this abyss
With no sight of relief, no spiritual rebirth.

I tussled raging waves with no arising shore.
I tussled while caged in this jail of soul demise.
I tussled, and despite the looming doom I sized,
I tussled to preserve my tenure as before.

But now that I barely see any horizon
On this long road traveled, this deceiving journey,
I will forsake the hands of the friends, the many
Who genuinely care, all baffled, with reason.

The crushing laziness befalling all my bones
Leaves me weakened and bare without a thought to hold.
Dreary and all worn out, I drag my blighted soul
Through the maze I crawled in, where darkness now long shone.

Maybe a tomorrow, for always appears one,
Manu militari, for thus resounds the need,
One will come from above, my inner spirit, feed,
But until this occurs, my life here is all done.

If Ever I Had

Alone, after a piece of choice
Written down one summer day long,
To my ears came a gifted voice
Performing such a lovely song.

Among the distorted lyrics,
I could perceive words and gathered
They were all thrown for one to seek
The hidden meanings they fathered.

Twas all about a young daughter's
Death and the still-grieving father
Who witnessed the senseless slaughter
Of a young child, treasured feather.

Twas a year after he was told
Of the passing of his own child.
The flow of tears he tried to hold,
For she looked innocent and mild.

She was used as a carrier
Of a deadly bomb that destroyed
Their quarter. Never sorrier
Had he seen a young mule deployed.

I just could not help but escape
And land in turf of my daydreams
And ever gently roll the tape,
Picturing what it would all seem

If I were to be so lucky
To be given a female child,
Precious pearl, always so frisky,
That would rearrange one's lifestyle.

I picture us all together
In a small house, cozy and calm.
It would be me and her brother;
Mother no more had any qualm.

She would have only known ten springs
And be the apple of my eyes.
The quiescence of life would ring
Loud as her occasional sighs.

I would be the parent most blest;
My daily life would be a breeze.
Of life I'd suffer any test
And bless God at her every tease.

In all my dreams she'd play a part;
At her chatter I would delight.
Her eyes lovingly would impart
Much-needed warmth and cheering light.

My only princess she would be
When together we'd take long walks,
Naming flowers and chasing bees
While sustaining our private talks.

I'd teach her love and tenderness
That lie in every human heart,
That each and every one you bless,
Karma returns you back its part.

Around my desk where she would hang,
She'd interrupt my train of thoughts
With her queries of teenage slang
And giggle when I'd capture naught.

Deep in her eyes I'd see my fate,
With tenderness inside aglow.
She'd have come to us to relate
Of the heavens' gentle love flow.

She'd be an angel in disguise
Sent to offset my many needs.
And everyone she'd mesmerize
With gentle wit and righteous deeds.

The deep desires of the hearts
Are fed to the soul in silence.
The spirit keenly just imparts
What it takes from its provenance.

They lie within the soul and surge,
Triggered by the least of events,
Then come alive and gently merge
To become vivid sentiments.

But I return to this old tune,
Morose, for still in my old age,
Upon the sand of my dry dune,
Just two male birds have made passage.

Styx Crossing

The sun over nature lounges heavy as lead,
Throwing darts of fire on everyone's forehead.
All over the meadows, life brews and freely basks
And runs over two feet, slowly grazes on four.
There, a lonely cottage, much more than once before,
Stands willing to tackle the task.

The clear hours offer to the lingering mind
To span way past this scene and grasp what it can find.
So to the happy hour where you gather and feast,
Where lively, drunken lads sing to love they once knew,
The lyrics come ad lib, trickling down to renew
All that for them has long forgotten to exist.

Whatever will happen when we cease to exist?
How will we fence our last before we leave the piste?
To die a lovely death sounds almost ludicrous.
The soul is then harassed by a large horde of foes
And, on uncharted ground, has to pay what it owes
To a specter lugubrious.

What a shivering stance for the gasping mortal!
He can see life evolve as playful and festal.
The birds sing; the lilacs, amid the summer day,
Glow as ever before. But he clenches his fists,
And the sea of torments seems to never desist.
They come to fetch his soul on this dreaded doomsday.

As a nurse, I have led many of my patients
Down this horrific trail with kindness and patience.
In the midst of the scene, hassled by darted prongs,
When all weary they lie, breathing a short recess,
With your words of comfort mitigating their stress,
Nothing undoes what they did wrong.

But deep within yourself, witnessing this ordeal,
You can't help but wonder the nature of their deal.
What is it that they see causing this trembling fright?
Have they opened the door leading down that hallway?
Have they perceived that light so bright coming their way?
Have scary faces come to perturb their weak sight?

O death, where is thy sting? Right here, as they could hear,
"I come, for time's at hand, away from life to steer
Your soul. Now then come and follow me to the raft.
No need for last goodbyes or tears of deep sorrow"
All uttered in a voice guttural and hollow.
And right then blows a frigid draft.

But everyone trembles when faced with this hour.
Everybody abhors the dread of its power.
Be you king or pauper, your time of Styx crossing
Is always distressing. One is never prepared
To depart from this world unless deeply is shared
A blessed love bond with the God of the living.

Saturn

New York deep in the fall offers to the blank mind
A lovely plate of themes as diverse as its leaves.
And if the thoughts wonder, thankfully they will find
Worthy nature riddles, well-known, hard to retrieve.

The overcast heavens nurtures melancholy,
And the cooler degrees tickle the intellect.
The psyche veers to God, the one and the only,
Such a wonderland could erect.

Like remnants of a dream still floating in the souls,
They appear as shadows, hard yet to decipher.
And though they would attempt, they just can't pay the toll
To rejoin the dark night that now values cipher.

In such a time as these, fostering reflection
One gently can evade, devoid of an escort,
And reach the such-chosen of the destination
In a most rapid of transport.

Be it love or hatred, famine or disaster,
Or human condition or futuristic doom,
Or the plight of the soul in the life hereafter,
One has his share of bones to gnaw away his gloom,

There intoxicated, with mind heavy laden,
Ponders at full throttle and ponders fair and square
And securely exiled in this chosen Eden,
Idles away with frozen stare.

Now that I well exposed this ever-troubling stage
Where one can play a clown as good as a winner,
Let me freely divulge the silent war I wage,
Mulling on what awaits afterlife the sinner.

For over and over, I catch myself at night
Knocking hard at the door of this dark mystery.
It carries me often down some horrific fright,
Alone in silent misery.

I perceive that the soul, led by the flown spirit,
Springs freely deep in space, regaining lost function.
It hovers a short while, roaming favorite streets,
And through pull is summoned for examination.

There it sees the meaning of its every action,
And deeply it regrets, facing consequences.
Life takes its true visage, far from given notion
By this cold world references.

At times they visit us as daring butterflies,
Frolicking all around the ones they truly miss.
Like trying to reveal and dismantle some lies,
They hover 'round us though repeatedly dismissed.

Well imbue as they are of the meaning of life,
They frantically attempt to call the attention.
But the teachings are here, and to rid us of strife,
We should heed the admonition.

But for the ones who failed, despite repeated calls,
To follow the precepts and to uphold the truth,
Those who so knowingly cause the others to fall
By seeking their own gain and some thrilling sweet tooth,

Those who never suffered and despised poverty
And did every gimmick to gain shady fortune,
Those, the proud and haughty, bereft of charity
Now they sing a well-different tune.

They go land on Saturn, a dark and icy globe.
They land deep in trenches unknown by us thus far.
In the far universe, with her rings as a robe,
She holds them all captives until freed of all tar,

Cleansed of every blemish reflecting their failings.
And until every cent to the just divine scale
Has been carefully paid, amid the loud bawling
And gnash of teeth, always exhale.

Saturn, this huge planet designed by the Maker
As dreaded asylum for the heavens' justice,
It spins at deadly speed as though to make bleaker
Its bare and cold surface where no one is novice.

Up in its atmosphere, unlike our dear rainbow,
Two gigantic circles speed around its center.
High and deep in its sky, purposely they don't glow
To trap what on their path enters.

Like a dark predator, it spins and holds hostage
Seven small golden spheres in its axles well caught.
The other galaxies for it all left the stage
And shiver from afar, perceiving some onslaught.

The warmth of our sun is unknown to its vault;
From such a far distance, it appears dull and pale.
There is no day or night, so its time just default
To a somber and frigid scale.

But what a dreadful thought to see the sweet heavens,
So bright and glorious, attesting divine love,
To enclose in some part. Oh! How fat is that chance!
Some soul sarcophagus with fence spinning above!

The thoughts of grey matter sometimes come out as such,
But quickly the reason should steer us far from them.
The love that God depicts in creation is much
Too pure even when He condemns.

If ever the elders, in secret reflection,
Had one day bear such thoughts, lost in troubling dismay,
I hope that just like me they had the reaction
To veer right in Your love, O Lord, and safely sway.

For the overcast sky weighing down the spirit,
Often when unaware, drags us into its shade.
Always at Your bright dawn, with bright sun in our streets,
Those somber thoughts away will fade.

My Good Lord

I take it, it is fitted
That we bolster nowadays,
That we, humans, are seated,
In charge of our future days.

We rely on the power
Of made-up machinery
And easily devour
The wealth of any country.

With sharp eyes deep in the skies,
We can scrutinize the earth;
The universe we can size
And, in all its corners, surf.

We elect country leaders
As we choose the clothes to wear.
And this earth's precious cedars,
When we see fit, down we tear.

We adore all that glitter,
And we name them true idols.
And around them we jitter,
Canonizing them with dolls.

We uphold what we can see,
Worship only all science,
And revere proficiency
Regardless of provenience.

But I treasure deep inside
And will choose in a heartbeat
To the god boasting with pride
The meek Lord on donkey seat.

To the strong god of Wall Street,
The god of weapons and swords,
The god endowed with ram feet,
I prefer my loving Lord.

The good Lord who speaks of love,
Who, out of sheer mercy,
Lets Himself sullied and shoved
As divine trade currency.

The good Lord who gives this love
To be shared among brethren,
Spreads it in the stars above,
Rings it in each love refrain.

This love, essence of nature,
Root of all rolling seasons.
This love that grows the pasture
Down the farthest horizon,

That mends every broken heart
To rebirth free of sorrow,
That mends every broken part
Of the wings of the sparrow.

The One who feeds multitude
While preaching of forgiveness,
The One who in solitude
Comes lonely souls to caress.

Surely over centuries
We've been given great notions,
But we bask in reveries
That they were our creations.

Erect and ever higher
We build up tall skyscrapers;
Soulless beings we so father
To charm up all our capers.

Tell me, what would life become
Devoid of love benefits?
Tell me, what blessed wisdom
Would keep the sun in its seat?

But we receive all from God
Who sustains the life He gives.
Breaking this saving accord
Would the universe deceive.

Private Utterance

"I'm so sorry," she said, "I don't want to bother.
Time spent with you lingers and offers its sweetness.
But I look and wonder. Your forehead is smoother.
Right there I understand you're thinking tenderness.

"Seeing you is a treat, but then again, I watch
That no one comes perturb this hour made for two.
You silenced the ringer so that nothing can match
With this train of your thoughts with seats for me and you.

"I try not to disturb the flow that I perceive
When you seem to listen carefully, intensely.
And when you rapidly jot down what you receive,
The sound of the keyboard in my ears rings jolly.

"But it's good to see you, that we breathe the same air,
That I fix you a meal, but please give me a glance.
Peek every so often so I can further bear
While you sit at your desk all caught in your word trance.

"But you remain enthralled in the realm of your flow,
And deep inside my heart, I feel a slight burden.
I want you in my world and can take any blow,
But for the love of us, glimpse at me now and then."

Woman's Love

On earth, nothing can compare
To the love of a woman.
The universe always shares
But keeps this away from men.

This love rhymes with tenderness
And takes roots from the heavens.
It trickles down and comes bless
As divine treat through romance.

The soul glitters from her glance,
All adorned with shiny glow,
For God saw way in advance
Her might realm on all sorrow.

The most precious of the stones
Glitters best next to her eyes,
And the most powerful throne
Worries every time she sighs.

The flower to the garden
Redresses the bleak aspect;
A woman in a man's den
Begets warmth, love, and respect.

The smallest of all the dreams
From woman draws inner drive;
She reigns as a central theme
On all levels of our lives.

The sun shines on us below,
Spreading cheers in every dome;
Woman's love with eyes aglow
Feeds the soul and warms a home.

Long, long before this era,
For this poor world salvation,
God chose woman viscera
To offset our perdition.

Thus, the most precious creature
Having roamed this blessed earth
Is a woman which features
Her sweet and most blessed girth.

She and I Both

Riding this uptown train, we, on the way to work,
Met one day, eye to eye. She, so proud; I, the jerk.
Thoughts ablaze, eyes on fire, in silence we exchanged
Muffled inquiries of each other's status.
Our eyes at each other's necks held on mordicus,
But this to us never seemed strange.

Just like two birds lost in a crowd of city fair,
We dangled up and down holding each other's stare,
Sustaining the queries, stifling every reply
That could under this light reveal the silent screams.
Deep in each other's eyes we could perceive our dreams,
But on faith we could not rely.

So we went through the stops, but no passenger dared,
By blocking our view, perturb this love affair.
It seemed as the first time that we had us noticed.
It seemed as the first time, but despite empty seats,
Nothing had permitted this lovely duel to quit.
Face-to-face we chose to insist.

No verbal cue offered, no touch, no wink, no sign;
Nothing ever revealed that one day she'd be mine.
And I would verify that though loud in her thoughts
She had quickly dispelled this clear story foretold.
She never imagined, race barriers put on hold,
We were the true love we both sought.

She

Meanwhile, in the crowd I stood;
Meanwhile, she stood at my side.
She unveiled an eager mood;
I trembled deep down inside.

The eve blew a gentle breeze;
The crowd cheered the playing game.
Two lovebirds offered a tease;
I kept silent just the same.

And her team won the first set;
Her eyes glowed in silent cheer.
I waved at a pal, and yet
She idled, willing and near.

I was fourteen and so shy;
She was fifteen and so prone.
The second set flew right by;
Her team won, and her joy shone.

She, lovely, queen of her class;
I, dorky, priming teenage.
She disposed to heed my pass;
I, too novice on this stage.

And the lovebirds' silent preach
Grew solid in the meanwhile.
The crowd clapped its joy at each
Volley serve given in style.

And she turned to me and smiled
In muted invitation.
In her eyes there was no vile
Or misguided intention.

Deep inside I felt so lost
In a mix of emotions;
The doom I fell in almost
And a surging elation.

She was beautiful and slim,
Had the whole world at her feet.
"Till we meet again, it seems,"
But she died … the short of it.

Evening Rowboat

Then we go on this rowboat,
With its sailor belching loud,
Gently gliding in the float
Amid the falsetto notes
Under this sky free of clouds.

Tis the ending of the day,
And we sit under the shade
From the sails. And loving rays
From your eyes come and display
Golden stars in sweet parade.

Right out loud the atmosphere
Revealing my love for you,
From the sailor's steady steer
To your heart I feel so near,
Connives with the sea deep-blue.

And the rocking of the waves
Gently lulling all our dreams
And removing every trave
Opens up all that I saved
Of plans with us as a theme.

I foresee the real burden
While you contemplate the joy.
I worry for now and then
Of problems we failed, laden,
But your faith can't be destroyed.

Humans strive until the end;
Of this life, it is the law.
No one lives without a hand
From a dear neighbor who lands
His support as a last straw.

We struggle on troubled sea,
Strong winds against the faces.
In the dark we try to see
The faint hope of His mercy,
For all frowns, God erases.

With sails torn from winds ablow,
We attempt to reach the goal.
Hell and high water below
Will never erase the glow
Of the target we uphold.

And we battle all the same
Under heavens' gentle watch.
Despite the burdens we tame
Or any flickering fame,
One by one we leave the batch.

All ends any given day;
All fades at the horizon.
Eat you flesh or eat you hay,
We all meet with a doomsday;
We all have a due season.

This day hits the meek and mild
And astounds the strong and proud
Regardless of what we piled
And the ideas we defiled,
We all go rot in a shroud.

Therefore, why all this unrest
And unending bickering?
Why not cater to love zest
And give no chance to the pest
Fanning human slandering?

For we feverishly work
Night and day like busy bees,
We wake and silently lurk,
With desires sharp as dirk,
On the mirages we see.

For the dream we so endear
And the prize we so treasure
Always are source of all fears.
They lead us with silent tears
To one's final departure.

For in His wisdom, God tests
His chosen at every turn.
The trials undergone attest
His love for us, at its best;
Child you love you do not spurn.

To the glorious warrior,
The meek wise man, He oppose'.
To the mighty dictator,
Rich and drunk of his grandeur,
He gives the adequate dose.

And to the lovely flower,
He says, "Glow as you see fit.
Shine to the world an hour,
For the sun will devour
Your petals, if fails the sleet."

As mortals, we try to fight
Against the order decreed
And the opponent we slight.
But always there will be might
To obstruct everyone's greed.

Whether we face it or not,
We all try to reach a mark,
But the ever-daring plots
Tip the scale where all the dots
Are obliged as blunt as stark.

All those fake pearls desired
Fade away before our eyes,
Consumed by life wildfires.
The only true sapphire
Is to have made love your prize…

So I bow in sheer silence
While you drill the stars above,
And from the sea wave cadence,
Inquire with persistence
The tomorrow of our love.

The answer remains untold,
But I hope for a clear sign.
The night landed clear and cold,
And as the sailor foretold,
The evening turned out just fine.

Let me dive in the abyss
And the muted wave tumult
While you, my endearing Ms.,
Enjoy the uncovered bliss
And thus let your soul exult.

If you gaze a bit longer
At this heavens' scenery
And ignore this brave singer
Right amid this star binger,
You'll take hold of God's glory.

The Spider and the Nettle

The lonely spider and dreaded nettle,
Of us both despised,
Forever battle, forever mettle,
Mindless of their size.

Sneakily and cursed, stunted and spindly,
Creeping on the ground,
Crawling from a tomb, knit exceedingly,
And the world, astound.

In the trap they weave, and the time they loom,
So deceiving state,
Just so they remain caught up in their doom,
Ever cheated fate.

Forever stranded and ever laden,
Cast out of rebate,
Malicious victims in abyss hidden,
Denied of debate.

Mother Nature gives and takes in return
To even the scores,
And so to the sting and so to the burn,
She sets the decor.

The scorn they beget and the fright they cause
To us all below
Blot out any thought and even oppose
A drop of sorrow.

But clear of their sights and free of their web,
Relief and solace,
They're still to nature, with or without neb,
God's created grace.

Under His Dome

Come see this majestic church
With dome high up in the sky,
With its roof where chose to perch
This bird's nest, so meek and shy.

Often in a large temple
With massive and deep ceiling,
Little birds there find ample
Safe place to nest their suckling.

Under the arch, little swifts
Gesticulating in moss,
Expect for some treasured gift
From the Savior on His cross.

Somber corners of the roof
Are ideal for them to grow,
And this shelter, weatherproof,
Caters to swift or sparrow.

The saints in glorious silence
Enjoy these two blessed worlds;
The faithful deep reverence
And the birds, true nature's pearls.

The Virgin, mother of all,
Seems to keep a tender gaze
On her flock seated in stalls
And her avian cubs in daze.

All the prophets still herald
The birth of the blessed child
While the birds quickly installed
New hay to the ones they piled.

And rings out the sacred hymn
Filling up this holy place
But resounds one precious theme:
God's love with His varied face.

Love Rebirth

Life recurs, my lovely child.
The gray sky sheds its pallor.
Here on earth where all is mild,
Human hearts expose valor.

Love trickles down all blessings
To smother human sorrow,
Makes sparkle all living things,
From the stars to the willow.

Old man winter now's all gone,
Dark season upon our stage.
Where tears from old dreams undone
Drench the made-over visage.

Far amid searing sorrow,
When the tears would come attest
The new dawn and clear morrow,
The lonely shows no protest.

The tree branches all-abloom,
All adorned with sprouting buds,
Tomorrow will shade the plumes
Of the sparrows sharing cuds.

The sweet dawn of yesteryear
Comes shine in your eyes anew.
It came chasing all our fears
And chased old man winter too.

And the loud laughter they throw
Brighten the faces you meet.
In the night, the stars aglow;
In the day, baby birds tweet.

Around, the rebirth displays,
On Nature's recurring grace,
Nurturing buds as they say
To lovebirds, "Come and embrace."

In the air, the balm enthralls.
You delight in their essence.
Basking softly in your stall,
I inhale better fragrance.

I rejoice under your charm;
In your eyes, I search my peace.
When you're sad, I'm all alarmed;
When you laugh, I find my bliss.

Mother Nature, conniving,
Offers to us lovingly
Riddles ever enchanting,
All granted surprisingly.

The heavens always reflect
In your eyes the bright of day;
Around us nothing objects
When in my arms you come stay.

And so we bathe all day long
In the midst of all these scents.
To nature we sing our song
For her treats so florescent.

Not a care to dull our bliss,
Not a thought to dent our mirth.
On a spring day such as this,
We're royalties on this earth.

And we share this elation
Around to every flower.
The sun strokes every section;
We delight in love power.

Hand in hand with one heartbeat,
We enjoy this precious care.
For the whole world at our feet,
We give thanks while it is there.

Cupid's most precise arrow
Seeks its prey through a dense crowd.
No sense ducking its shadow
When of faith you're so endowed.

Every flower in the spring
In April gloats lovingly.
But always when May bells ring,
They fade so annoyingly.

But you bring heaven's goodness,
So around you I hover.
When you leave, a blunt sadness
Is the trade felt all over.

And your hands cradle my soul
From heaven so far away.
When you leave, I lose control,
Sensing the setting dismay.

I follow your every step
To your dear shadow so strung.
The sweet sound of your footsteps
Beats the best song ever sung.

When all weary and jaded,
I rely on your courage.
From your font, for me slated,
I remedy my shortage.

Love infuses deep inside
The heaven's felicity.
This spark you can hardly hide
Divulges infinity.

Without your gaze, I stifle
And lose my innermost drive.
I go my way and shuffle;
How painful it is to thrive.

I exhale with somber sighs
Of my world so disengaged.
I forsake the least of ties;
All around seem so unstaged.

And I yearn for your return
To come breathe your life in me.
Deep inside I feel the burn,
Heart pounding and hands clammy.

What else can I ever need?
What again can stir my fright?
Close to you I bask indeed,
Exult when I hold you tight.

You're the sole reason I pray
Either grateful or begging.
You're my heart's God-given prey;
You alone I'll be hunting.

All around I go and shout
Of your blessed tenderness;
And I see daffodils pout
When I mention your finesse.

And when they all inquire
About this living fairy,
I'll stutter under fire,
Lost for words, my sweet chérie.

Next to me, promise you'll stay,
Lest you seal my slow demise.
To this world I'm just a stray
Without your joy as my prize.

Life offers ever freely
The most precious of its gems.
Love renders ever jolly
Every soul that from it stems.

Let us remain so grateful
To the Giver of all grace.
Let us be ever hopeful
And pray that we keep His pace.

Love's Stead

Winter spreads out its frosted coat
And preys over all living souls.
In the air, hatred thinly floats;
Nature mournfully pays the toll.

The universe offers one shade,
Resting in a dim glare of light.
Secure inside what could evade
Lest you suffer under this plight.

But open up and let it flow;
From your heart let your love exhale.
The sky for now has lost its glow;
Shine your love since the world's all pale.

Doubting besets the human race
And weakens all flow of merits.
But if you fail the Source of grace,
At least believe its benefits.

Believe in this love He bestows
That shines through the nights and the days.
Believe this never-ending flow
That bursts with the sun's dawning rays.

Open your heart to love and hope,
Open your heart where I reside.
Glide down on my rhyme silky slope,
And in my arms come and abide.

Daily, in this vale we journey;
Worthy actions blot all failings.
Mercy with or without money
Expunges all wicked dealings.

Bask on the beauty deep within
That permeates your loving eyes.
Make love your theme of daily scene;
Let it cause all hatred demise.

To every ounce of bitterness,
Counter your subtlety of love.
Expose your flame of gentleness
And your candor of gentle dove.

A bitter heart is cold as ice;
Remain ablaze deep in your core.
With your bright smile, your world, entice
And rekindle your dull decor.

Like stars shining in the North Pole,
Keep your heart glowing with your love.
Attune your traits of inner soul
To the stead of the sky above.

Rarest of Pearls

Against all odds, let your heart blaze.
Let hope shine through your darkest nights.
Love comes always with dawning rays,
While hope repels the darkest frights.

Love brings the sea to kiss the shore,
Tells the wind to reshape mountains.
Love brings the stars to heaven's door;
Creation's grace subtly sustains.

Love begets dreams; love nurtures life.
Love opens doors to golden bliss.
Love guides the soul through any strife
And restores mirth that glory missed.

Through thick and thin, let your love show.
Through thick and thin, let your soul soar.
Dare and the world around will know
The treasures deep within your core.

Love when your sun forgets to shine.
Radiate your own warmth around.
Follow your heart, follow the Vine,
Let His sap in your branch abound.

Day after day, let your love grow
Under the care of the Spirit.
Since what you reap is what you sow,
You'll amass spiritual merits.

Allow God's love to flow through us.
Allow His kingdom to beset
His Spirit gifts who makes pious
To original sin offset.

Inspiration is often sought.
We retrieve it from all that blooms
From this garden that the Lord wrought
To day by day our souls to groom.

So be my muse, O divine treat!
Let me reflect on your beauty.
Let me rejoice, come take a seat
Till I reach my satiety.

Humble minds have but one solace
That trickles down from divine bliss.
Upon their knees they get the grace
That the so proud ones always miss.

Therefore, my never-ending quest
Mirrors the ever-golden truth.
Everything else I reject lest
I lose my every single tooth.

So I delight in the somber
Rewards that slowly you disclose.
The proud and boasting encumber
The Spirit flow to those He chose.

For all the pomp is meaningless
And, in His bright sun, melts away.
Love and its blessed tenderness
Keep all our troubling pains at bay.

All the fleeting pleasures at reach
Seem to deflate before our eyes,
And we stand there searching the glitch
That we appraised, stole our dear prize.

And love remains as sole anchor
On the dark sea we sail over.
It's the seal of the Creator,
A soothing balm like no other.

No matter the many crosses
That might have burdened your shoulder,
Keep ashine all divine glosses
That reflect from your soul's boulder.

Troubling Years

What if I were to say,
Before you're on your way,
What I want you to know?
Been sometimes on my mind,
But I could never find
The adequate lingo.

And if you let me talk
Before you take your walk,
Hopefully you'll muster
The strength to forgive me
And of this infamy
Get me off the roster.

Troubling years,
Childish years,
The time at hand is so precious.
Troubling years,
Carefree years,
We were young and impetuous.

In my college those days,
We were all, as they say,
Pretending we're students,
Just experimenting
On any given thing
That could cause a constraint.

Nothing was out of reach,
And all around we'd preach
Of this so-called power
That we thought was our own
And put us on this throne
Of that sandy tower.

Troubling years,
Thrilling years,
School at the time was such a drag.
Troubling years,
Bubbling years,
To the world I was such a nag.

All day we fooled around,
Causing tears, causing frown
To everyone 'round us,
And when we were monished
For whatever we'd breached,
We'd yell it was not just.

Then I had to repeat,
From lack of school spirit,
Many of my levels
And was justly expelled
For having freely failed;
Against all rules, rebelled.

Troubling years,
Painful years,
We never saw coming our doom.
Troubling years,
Stressing years,
Block after block we sealed our tomb.

But the worst came later,
A troubling disaster
When I fathered my son
For the gut-wrenching fear
Fostered so many tears,
Sealing my faith thereon.

But a lifetime it took
To retrieve from my book
The blessings well hidden;
I surely would have died
For too weak, would have tried
Illicit drugs at hand.

Troubling years,
Wretched years,
Should I sober my time wastage?
Troubling years,
Carefree years,
For my wisdom, you set the stage!

Wisdom

Resplendent, unfading is glorious wisdom
And readily perceived by those who seek her side.
To the ones who love her, she offers jolly rides
And hastens to disclose and reveal God's kingdom.

He who watches for her at the mere crack of dawn
Shall not, in his lifetime, fail to gaze her treasures.
Far from disappointment he'll fall in the rapture,
For taking thoughts of her is prudence on a throne.

For he who wakes for her shall ultimately bask,
For she seeks on her rounds those of her care, worthy.
Then in blessed mercy, she rewards her trophy.
With all solicitude, makes them fit for all task.

Magical Night

June dusk with somber coat spreads all over the vale.
The sun draws its curtains, calls it a day, subtly.
The fragrances tickle, and the hearing unveils;
All senses are alert while we slumber lightly.

The stars are bright ashine in this eerie twilight,
Where the confused shadows waver under the skies.
They wonder what to trust: the dawning of daylight
Or the lingering dusk with heaven-sharing ties.

Love…Again

From this dreary vale of tears
Where you lay your weary head,
Don't expect your bliss, my dear;
Let your heart radiate instead.

This tabernacle of love,
Guiding us so steadily
Through the misleading shades of
That, to God, is pure folly.

We go forth as living tree
Whose sap fails before we bloom
And live life so wild and free
That we reap sadness and gloom.

We all long for happiness
With hope brewing deep inside.
It fuels never-ending quests
For clouds where sweet bliss abides.

But misery always looms
At every turn of our life
To subtly instill its doom
In the stem of every strife.

Nothing's amiss but sorrow,
And the dancing horizon
Always displays in soft glow
Blissful treats in all seasons.

The dawn of hope thus lingers,
Unveiling what we hold dear
Where the sun's golden fingers
Sketch the prizes not so near.

Reflecting, against all odds,
The treasures of heaven's bliss,
So the soul gratefully nods
For prompting as clear as this.

They come as flawless visions
Offered to this failing world,
Drawing every attention
Away from these so fake pearls.

They stand, given blessed shades,
From heaven trees bestowing;
They stand, and the soul parades
Amid soft leave-shuddering.

This reflection stands alone,
Attesting heavenly bliss.
We long for this precious stone,
Rare pearl that we often miss.

Reach as high, if you so dare;
Humanhood's hefty burden.
Dreaming, to souls, brings repair
When the body is laden.

The Ultimate Sacrifice
Blotted original sin.
Cross bearing, we pay our price
With love brewing deep within.

This love we spread all around
Will extenuate all prongs.
Through love, charity abounds;
Through love, we right all our wrongs.

Together, to its solace,
Let us thrive all day, all night.
To, one goal together, chase
With one hope solid and bright.

In this world of make-believe,
I would gladly bear my cross,
Knowing that I can retrieve
From you all dreams I once lost.

The Sole Destination

On the fresh lawn in the forest
Eases the hunter, all adream.
Amid shadow-dancing contest,
He fails to catch what it all seems.

The ever-vigilant soldier,
Over his battlefields, ponders,
But not a thought is lovelier
Than his Jenny's smiling candor.

And the longing, lonely shepherd
Caresses the thought deep within
Of seeing multiply his herd
To marry the lovely Jeanine.

So take a good look all around
And see how precious is a dream.
It nurtures the hope where life pounds
And mirrors the soul's silent screams.

Relentingly though yet eager,
The poet roams all over the world.
With sharp mind and body meager,
Gathers moss, flowers, and rare pearls.

See the seaman down on his knees,
So tired of the foamy waves,
Imploring heavens for mercy
To see the shores for which he craves.
When all alone on the dark sea,
The waves hammer the wasted boat.
The jolly scenes that he foresees
Bring back the pub and jolly notes.

And see the priest in devotion,
Meditating over his flock.
He prays for heartfelt conversion
With hope as solid as a rock.

See the many who on their minds
Carry the weight of their own sphere
And so ever attempt to find
A way for it to safely steer.

And the nursing mother beholds
Her precious child, her sole treasure,
Shielding it from upcoming cold,
Shielding it from life's exposure.

They all bear hidden deep inside
A yearning Word, a hungry feel,
So staggering that they can't hide;
It keeps their lives rooted and real.

Each one has its own objective
Based solely on the divine plan.
Each one struggles not to deceive
Each time they feel it strong and plain.

It comes bouncing deep in their dreams;
It's a call they cannot ignore.
It comes mostly with subtle screams
But always surges from the core.

It gives a meaning to one's life,
Keeping one's spirit on its toes.
It rings out the sighs so rife
That's so obvious to friends and foes.

It permeates in all aspects
Of one's life and deep-anchored traits.
It's universal and affects
Continents, states, oceans, and straits.

Whether dimmed or brightly gleaming,
It shines for the whole world to see.
The sun attests in its shining
And makes it dance on shiny seas.

You can perceive it in nature,
When the brook runs, when the birds coo.
It's loud and clear and is treasured
In the cradle and the tomb too.

This Word resets nature each time
The spring comes ringing at its door.
It despises nickels and dimes
And freely gives what's in its stores.

It roams over meadows and ponds
And to their shudders gives essence.
It thrills each time little birds bond,
Expands with every rose fragrance.

It's the strong burst in every sail
Taking small boats on their journey.
The tidal sea follows its trail,
And stars at night it makes shiny.

Ever eternal is this Word,
Foundation of heaven and earth.
Through faith, it begets heaven's pearls;
Through love, it sheds its lasting mirth.

For love itself makes us able
To boldly face the come what may,
To humbly carry the feeble,
To shed the light along our way.

Love opens up, from heaven's gate,
The treasured light of the Spirit,
Bestowing gifts from God's estate,
Bestowing love as divine treats.

Love comes abide deep in the hearts
And warms the soul in sweet rapture.
The Holy Spirit's seven darts
Spread lasting fruits, with good measure.

It creates bonds between two souls,
The kind that binds your heart with mine.
They get to chat in a big shoal;
They get to chat of things divine.

As the window lets the sun through
And puts in display what's hidden,
God's love will make all dreams come true
Without a doubt, my sweet maiden.

He creates them, man and woman,
Endows them with a leading heart.
In it they keep all His commands
That keep them from falling apart.

While in journey in this here vale,
Far from the Source of all that's good,
They can behold, although yet pale,
The God, giver of daily food.

As nature basks under the sun
And comes alive in the summer,
So love and prayer daily stun,
Making the souls shine like glimmer.

Since the whole world chose to follow
Whatever tickles their senses,
Let us love so we can borrow
Strength from heaven for defenses.

Thus, it's never too late for love
To come crashing upon the shore.
God never fails from up above
To lighten loads, to even scores.

Nature's Secret

A bright sunshine's aglow and warm;
A jovial spring day whiles around.
All amid this abandoned farm,
Life of all kind jitters abound.

Over the pond's peaceful waters,
Dragonflies' ever-peering eyes
Scan feverishly their quarters
For other non-friendly life signs.

The budding roses all abloom,
To hummingbirds ever daring,
Bask in the sun, devoid of gloom,
While to the breeze, gently swinging.

Nature out loud blesses the Lord.
Everywhere shouts of Gloria
Resound from joyful, sweet accords
Or spring from muttered euphoria.

The muffled sounds of the forest
Yet portray vivid sceneries;
See the fawns in skipping contest,
See beetles in humble queries.

The moon glimmers, pale diadem,
Over the hill's bright greenery.
She shows silently where life stems,
Safely blessing this true fairy.

And wallflowers with golden locks
Caress tenderly the brick wall,
And old furrows from laden trucks
Gladly become sprouting seed stall.

And love freely spreads its blessings
From this blue sky to every trench.
The sun, through door ajar, beaming;
The shadow soothing the old bench.

In the fresh air, all breathe aright,
The forest chats and the grass lawns…
Brothers don't fear; sisters don't fright;
From nature's breath, the secret's flown.

Sweet Nothings

When I hark of your prowess,
I smile subtly yet sadly.
What with your deep faith, you bless,
Seems to me utter folly.

Vain Glory's often dethroned
By Envy's blazing banner.
The seeds the latter has sown
Never meet the poor gleaner.

Success always flies away;
Power's ever eluding.
But Love, all her cares convey
So often with sweet nothings:

All I long for is your smile
And the sweet sound of your voice
And see nature as she whiles
Or your eyes as preferred choice.

Please don't take away from me
The glow of my guiding light.
In glory or infamy,
Your sweet name soothes all my nights.

Under your angelic gaze
Where I bask my life away,
Heavenly treasures ablaze,
Yet your love lightens my way.

All the thoughts that I carry,
Concealed in my gray matter,
In one accord did agree
To make you their sole chatter.

Your voice that I long to hear
Jingles softly in my heart
And magically away steers
All tumult the world imparts.

I dive in the ecstasy
Where I linger in daydreams,
And under my skull chassis,
Your name muffles all my screams.

If ever given the choice
To be king of this whole world,
For the sweet sound of your voice,
I'll forsake diamonds and pearls.

All ponds of divine treasure
Gleaming in the hereafter
In my heart would not measure
To the chime of your laughter.

Therefore, let me at your feet
Spread the mantle of my love
And bestow all loving treats
That you're yet unaware of.

Sweet angel with gaze aglow,
Fair lady of drowning tears,
Chase away all my sorrow,
Cast away my silent fears.

To The Concerned

As long as the heavens hover above us all,
As much as in nature resounds its sheer goodness,
To every living soul, shout your demented call.
Whisper to the youngsters; sustain them in their falls,
Remind the proud elders of wisdom, the richness.

Show them the horizon closing in day by day.
Beyond the troubled sea where we all navigate.
Tell of the golden crown that chastity displays;
Tell the crowd of the truth of which they should not sway.
Speak of the days to come and of the pearly gate.

In each and every word, with any given rhyme,
Reveal the blessed truth that so much they distort.
Allow that the reader, at any given time,
Regains treasured solace and recovers their prime.
Relay from God above to each soul some comfort.

Sing to them how precious this given life can be;
Remind them that on earth, nothing is made to last;
That thanks to God above, what matters is still free;
That always when we ask, He shows us His mercy
And He waits for us all after this here life's past.

So there, in your alcove under heaven's curtain,
Blessed inspiration flowing between your lines,
Convey to the poor world what is sure and certain.
And maybe from chaos, divine peace they'll obtain
And on this long journey avoid the buried mines.

From God Through Nature

Summer's the season of all grace;
Summer's the season of fire.
The warmer weather brings solace
For spirits to soar much higher.

See the night skies of sapphire
Followed by day bright and merry.
In the evening, all retire
In gatherings loud and cheery.

The trees bask in every aspect
With the warm and nurturing sun,
And the balmy shades they project,
In blessings, are second to none.

They all welcome whosoever
From daily labors wants to rest;
Heaven's relief to the toiler
And nature comfort at its best.

They provide soothing oasis
When the radiant day is scorching
And open up the dreamy bliss
That repairs all human failings.

There, human nature comes alive,
Merging to golden reverie;
From the winter, all so deprived,
It bashfully steers to fairy.

And everywhere they freely hang
Sprouting buds and blooming flowers
To redecorate in a bang
The deep trenches, the tall towers.

The opulent shows in display
Of fragrance and colors alike
Proudly showcase and loudly say
That summer's here so spirits spike.

The flowers mingle all around
And hand in hand fling their beauty.
Some resurfacing the warm ground,
Some exploding in sheer gaiety.

Even the old shack's wooden roof
Regains its mossy appearance;
It stands erect as solid proof
Of show of flowers' true radiance

Where you see in the subtle shade,
Deep in the aspects of its dome,
Young spiders numbly giving trade
Through the many roses they roam.

And quietly, deep in the heart,
All filled with blessed tenderness,
Humble souls thankfully take part
To the Lord's display of goodness.

They thank for the breath of fresh air.
They thank for the warmth all around.
They thank for weather clear and fair
As well as for birds' jolly sounds.

So if awakes the destitute
Down on his knees and full of hopes,
The deep-blue sky, as to the mute,
Reminds him, "It's not time to mope.

"That under the blessed heaven,
To God everything is the same.
That the eagle and the raven,
Both can call to His blessed name.

"Under my dome and its degrees,
I provided for your parents.
For them living was not a breeze.
I appeased most of their torments.

"I poured over their humble graves
The dew for a rich lawn to grow.
Come claim the wealth that I have saved.
Come see all that for you I sow.

"Come and gather from my vineyard.
Come and sample from my garden.
Come take a much-careful regard
At what most of the world disdains.

"To me it matters that you smile.
To me it matters that you glow.
Your parents have longed for a while
Of your laugh to hear the echo."

The poor soul heeded the advice,
Shunning the load on his shoulders.
He didn't ask to be told twice,
Dashed amid roses and heathers.

Amid nature where all is free,
Free the flowers and free the fruits,
Free the rest under shady trees
And laughing birds in sweet pursuits.

The still pond reflects his image;
The world around nudges his soul.
Everything speaks the same language
Where love, the hand of freedom, holds.

The once-dreadful night's now so kind.
Wrapped in its shadowy blanket,
He sleep-leaves all worries behind
To be the stars' favorite pet.

"Don't let a thing bother your rest,
For you will spring up with God's grace!"
The moon won't put you to the test
As does the sun in its embrace.

*She is so much, much more gentle
And cradles toils, cradles sorrow.
She keeps us under her mantle,
While the sun our faces, burrows.*

*When the warbler attends her nest,
Well hidden from weather caprice,
And when nature regains her zest
After suffering heaven's piss.*

*While awake in my lonely nights,
Silently I always picture
That the rewards of winter's plights
Were redeemed by Mother Nature.*

*She suckles her many offspring
Under watch of the Creator,
But she favors those suffering
As does the most blessed Savior.*

*With calm and peaceful composure,
She offers to the afflicted
Treasures beyond any measure,
Not what to which he's addicted.*

*The fruit to ease his hunger pangs,
The brook to quench his thirst after.
The sun his shivering, to prang,
All needs for which he may falter.*

Then July slowly expires;
Summer mournfully weeps away.
Trees drop leaves with shades of fire
As they, side to side, slowly sway.

And October subtly stumbles,
Slowly losing its golden coat.
And shivering willows mumble
Same prayers that last year they wrote.

Armies of clouds with fierce thunder
Chase summer so relentlessly.
Striking lightning puts asunder
The remnants of warmth fearlessly.

The lonely indigent shudders,
For winter shoves show no mercy.
The cold, day after day, plunders,
Causing a dire urgency.

Crushed all the dreams, flown all the hopes,
Darkness emerges all around.
No fruits, no sunshine on the slopes,
The whole world dies without a sound.

He sobs and sobs over nature
All covered up with sheets of frost.
As he readies to self-immure,
He hears the clear voice of a ghost.

This luminous angelic being
Gazes tenderly on the poor man.
Of Hope and Faith, the third sibling,
She comes swiftly to land a hand.

"I am godsent. I'm Charity.
I am here to lighten your load.
When your world's short of clarity,
I'll go along you on the road!

"I come to dwell in your alcove
Devoid of any warmth at all.
On your knees, to the God above,
In the ears all petitions fall.

"I come to lessen your concern.
I come, sent to the ones in need!
I come for your Father discern'
Your distress, so I come with speed!

"I cater to one's secret will
And offer much-needed solace.
The sender, of blessings I fill.
The grantee, of blessings I grace."

O sweetness, O blessed comfort!
O living source of divine grace!
Reflect of celestial resort,
Angel with deep feminine trace!

When the soul readies for its flight
Yet lacks the least human support,
She stands as soothing cheer in sight;
She stands just as divine comfort.

In the dead of old man winter,
When the shivers clinch mandibles,
She goes around, gently mutters
The groans and moans still audible.

She visits shacks, hovels, hutches,
Spreading around divine relief.
The many goodies she clutches
Bring in the cheers, chases the grief.

And the soothing warmth of fires
Restores the hopes in the bosoms.
If it were placed any higher,
The sun to the blind would come home.

She also gathers little ones
Lost in the dark, deep street corners.
They gather, for being alone
Would of this world make them goners.

The most cherished in her esteem
Are the lost ones, the meek and poor.
They are in her eyes the ones deemed
To get most of heaven's downpour.

She cradles their sweet innocence,
Consoles and lulls their nakedness.
She kisses away the offense
Done unto their soul's sinlessness.

And while she smothers their hunger
And wipes their teary, sullied face,
She finds a reason to linger
And tenderly keeps up their pace.

And if ever it so happens
That a rich person comes around,
Be he brethren, be he heathen,
She nudges them from their deep frown.

For they're the ones the most in need,
The misers. The ones so many
Who could, the poor, easily feed,
But Heavens feels the irony.

"Woe to whosoever revels,
Basking around loud and merry,
When on his very next level
Starves a young one from penury.

"Nothing indeed is more fatal
Than to see people's airiness.
A cozy hall so much festal,
A host so proud of his richness.

"And in the midst of much excess,
With frenzy and choices of wine,
This heavy load of emptiness
Crushes the branches of the Vine.

"Share the bounty and share the joy.
Give to improve your soul's tenure.
Give so God's blessings to enjoy.
Give so God's mercy to incur.

"Blessed are they who give freely!
Giving amounts divine treasures.
Give alms and the soul merrily
Savors hidden divine pleasures.

"Blessed is he who lovingly
Attends the needy in his midst.
The tears he dries so gracefully
Will quench all fires on his piste.

"Nothing sheds more blessings on he
Whose kindness befalls the children.
Their voices reach God's ears, and He
In turn, rewards the true brethren.

"Almsgiving standing on love's sake
Will make the giving hand prosper.
The vase of love can never break
Once the clay trusts in the potter."

And the seasons will come and go,
But faith in God should always grow.
He ever minds the seeds He sow'
And gently eases their sorrow.

He shed His blood, the world to save,
And His kinship remains offered
To good willers as to depraved
Upon this cross where He suffered.

He sheds His everlasting treats
Even on those who freely choose
To shun His message and forfeit
His heart so loving and enthused.

The more they despise His sweet yoke,
The more merciful He remains.
And their hard hearts He always pokes,
Hoping they hear His love refrain.

He is the mighty king of love
Who chose as a throne a manger.
Now He descends as a sweet dove
To free their hearts from all danger.

Under the snares of the dear foe,
He offers freedom with His Word.
He always hears the faint echo
Of bleeding hearts' unspoken words.

So when panting under burdens,
Know for certain He sees it all.
He knows what's to be cross laden;
Under it, many times did fall.

He is the ever-living God
Who in His palm holds the whole world.
In Him we can find safe abode
For meek souls to freely unfurl.

So in the midst of life's turmoil,
When we feel lost and all downcast,
With ears of faith, although we toil,
We hear His promise it won't last.

For through it all, the sufferings,
The seasons, the years, days, and nights,
Mother Nature will always bring
The love of God in all His might!

His mercy carries no boundary,
And always all over the earth,
To His children, in a hurry,
God brings solace, blessings, and mirth!

Just Because

Just because every living soul
The Lord creates
Silently hungers to be whole,
Seeking a mate.

Just because every free motion
Thus extended
Is good or bad in reaction,
Forth intended.

Just because nature in the spring
Appears renewed.
Just because the night brings snoring,
Bad dreams all strewed.

Just because the golden sunshine
Brings happiness;
Just because with your hand in mine
I feel no stress.

Just because on every tree branch
Can a bird nests
And that every given park bench
Can love attests.

Just because every given brook
Quenches willows,
That all it took was just one look
For me to know

That all I needed in my life,
Genuine and true,
Was for you to decide and dive
And start anew.

To you only my thoughts aspire,
Mumbling your name
And my soul blazes in fire,
Your face to blame.

I send you silent well-wishes,
Riding my love,
Praying that the Lord enriches
You with His dove.

I send you all my ecstasy
With strolling dreams,
Each harboring a fantasy
Where you're the theme.

Yet still my mind has one island
With golden shore
Where it lingers, holding your hand
Like once before.

Receive my love, my angel fine,
For rainy days.
Your hand is already in mine,
Thus the Lord says.

My Better Half

From that very first day that you dared quench my thirst,
From that very first day on me you set your glance,
From that very first day that you came to adjust
The realm of my poor soul longing for a last chance.

From that very first day that softly, in my arms,
You whispered in my ears your winged melody.
From that very first day that you gently disarm'
My solitary stance, my heart shy yet rowdy.

From the very first day that in my night I saw
My shining guiding light reflect straight from your eyes.
From the very first day, under bind of no law,
My soul came to shiver at the least of your sighs.

I now have come this far, although standing alone,
With no chime of your voice, with no charm of your grace,
Still branded by your smile, and proudly can intone
That always will my soul ever dwell in your place.

No sparkling spring chicken, no well-rounded cupcake,
No foreign Madonna will my queen dare dethrone.
In the warmth of her gaze, my heart will always bake;
In the realm of her love, my soul will bask alone.

The Feast of Life

The magnificent hall harbors the huge table;
The buffet stretches out. The servers well able,
With gliding mastery, refresh glasses and plates.
Nothing is omitted that tickles the palates.
The shiny silverware and the sparkling crystals
Adorn with elegance tablecloths of Nepal.
In the great atmosphere marking this royal feast
Rings out an orchestra interpreting Franz Liszt.

Of the human species, you can meet a spectrum:
Races, gender, and age. Young lads tall and handsome;
Young folks full of laughter and old folks of breath short.
Young ladies, fair and plum, giggling happy cohort.
And everybody slurps, and everybody eat.
Everybody wiggles their butts into their seats.
The mouths chew and babble and much too fast swallow;
Some eat for the whole year; others just can't follow.

The statues all frozen, here and there in the hall,
Seem so taken aback by this gluttony ball.
The sketches hanging tall, much too afraid to talk,
Appear to far away find something else to stalk.
The uninvited guests, the ones buzzing away,
Every now and then fly sampling all the food trays.
Thereafter, when all filled from whatever they picked,
They dive into the drinks, dipping right in their beaks.

Flags of every credo, hanging high, hanging proud,
By the many insects are used as living shroud.
They dance nonchalantly to the blow of the fans,
Rocking baby spiders yet devoid of their fangs.
And as it seems to go, every living creature
In this lively cosmos takes part in this rapture.
And the food comes around brought by gallant garçons,
Followed by empty trays emptied in unison.

And rings out from the hall an all-festive climate
Where every living soul enjoys its joyous fate.
Life is lived at its best, and nothing can go wrong.
Everyone's a winner, be you weak, be you strong.
If ever God exists, He is right here tonight
And basks in happiness at this merry hall sight.
They all have been blessed and were summoned today
To be here together and loudly feast away.

So they shine all aglow in this gorgeous evening
Where everyone's a queen looking for her own king.
Power intoxicates and makes a man a fool,
Lulled into the belief that the world's his stepstool.
Not a thought can hinder this heartfelt elation;
Not a word can alter these fine conversations.
And the reluctant host, stealthy and vigilant
To most healthy portions, his wide-open smile grants.

But unfortunately, excess nullifies greed;
There's only one stomach in one day one can feed.
If one so much ignores this organ's desperate calls,
The conscience comes around and in the mind installs
A big load of burdens that eclipse all your joy.
But for a bunch of us, the conscience just annoys.
Cleverly we deploy to her clear attention
A group of strong vices for her demolition.

And in the midst of all the loud, crackling laughter,
The petty talks around, the gossiping chapters,
The drinks served much too soon, the desserts, the sherbets,
The arousing music from the skillful experts,
With all the lovely dames giggling and offering
To all the handsome lads their most precious screening,
And the servants too keen at filling the crystals,
And the spirits rising, blurring all reason's calls,

No one perceived the knock persistent yet subtle
Of the somber fellow who rushed at full throttle.
He had, from what he said, a most pressing message
That must be delivered with no leading presage.
And when they let him in, all dressed in somber coat,
Nothing could have hinted the content of his note.
He went up the stairway, down the long corridor,
Headed for the great hall once he opened the door.

The shivering coldness that embraced this great hall
Has been felt in the past or never felt at all;
It all depends, of course, on years of experience.
He wavered for a while, weighing the large audience,
Then Death, that was his name, turned into a dark cloud
And glided so slowly over meek, over proud,
And when he found his prey, all drunk and face stuffing,
He quickly grabbed his soul… left his spirit sleeping.

The Hourglass

See, amid the thick clouds the king star retire.
And the darkness settles. The thunderstorm will rage
Over this here nature whose dampened attire
Will welcome other days and other nights will stage.

And bright days will arise by quiet nights followed,
To change, as they always, of nature every trench.
Forests, valleys, mountains will gradually furrow;
Brooks and rivers alike into the sea will branch.

Nature will sprout anew, lovely buds to garnish,
And through given seasons will display love around.
Trees will come and will go and with time will blemish
But never will resist bird's nests to stem abound.

And the years will amount, followed by other springs;
The seasons in cascade will bring us joy or pain.
Nature will forever remake her facial rings
All under the same chime of the church bell refrain.

But with a slow decline, I bend my grayish brow
Closer toward the earth, laden but yet so glad.
To the dust where I sprang, my ultimate burrow,
I'll return peacefully the matter I once had.

The Science of Giving

You wake up all groggy, eyes bloodshot and all stoned,
Unaware of the day or the place, and you groaned
From the searing headaches born from this dark abuse
Of all the substances your body pants under,
Which sooner or later will take it asunder,
To live another day of this life you misuse.

The non-ending parties, the loud friend gatherings,
The glitters, the good food, the dancing, the snorting;
The coition binging with anything that breathes,
The planes, the fancy cars, and the admiration
Of the frenzied groupies begging for attention,
Your ego-wheedling thus receive.

But in the midst of all these blasting enjoyments,
Have you once considered the unspoken torments
That befall the homeless who perceives your fiestas,
The one at the corner on the cardboard sleeping,
Suffering cold and rain and the dear crowd sneering,
When just a meal from you would've eased his siesta?

His children are long gone, while friends on you hover.
You sleep in fine linen; only his clothes cover
His sullied, frail body from basic needs lacking.
Your blasting noise boring through the wax in his ears
Drowns every thought you have of your God-given fears;
Your world perception thus blocking.

Sadly, this world offers to the unprepared ones
Riches beyond compare with enjoyments in tons.
They miss the chance offered to offset their failures.
They ignore the teachings of the branches and Vine
And numb their inner voice with fine choices of wine
To happily cradle their dark wells of pleasures.

How blessed would it be, one day for you, rich bunch,
If your least of excess would be the poor one's lunch!
From your voluptuous drunkenness arising,
Instead of just binging, you would share your surplus.
For although in this world spring the minus and plus,
One should practice true thanksgiving.

The show of gratitude for what you so squander
Could reface your karma, if you take close gander.
Giving is the essence of this life you borrow';
Giving tickles the soul and enthralls the spirit.
Giving has the power to erase demerits
That weigh on all of us at the great tomorrow.

There, in the hereafter, where all is said and done,
Where the accounts are changed by nothing and no one,
Where the Lord of all lords and sole Maker of ghosts
Will refrain to your ears all His beatitudes,
Sadly you'll realize how your blunt attitude
Caused you your damnation the most.

Feed the poor, as He says, clothe the naked around.
The world's a better place when charity abounds.
If for the poor body; so one sleeps, so he dines,
The soul feasts and gets strong mostly by almsgiving.
Give in blessed silence, far from people prying,
For hence earthly praises rob the soul of its shine.

Spread your kindness around, your soul upgrade to thrive.
Give to the little ones, the so many deprive'.
Give so that in return blessings trickle galore
Down your posterity, the ones you hold so dear.
Then world calamities away from them will steer
Since the Lord's mercy you implore.

Give alms always; give alms, for always your kindness
In the blessed heavens amounts your true richness.
Give so to bring a smile to the face it comforts.
Give so to change your world one poor soul at a time.
Give so that in return you get your precious prime.
Give so that you improve your ultimate report.

Give for the main reason that it is the teaching
Brought to us lovingly by the Lord of all things.
And who knows, one clear day when dumbfounded you'll stand,
All contrite for the good that you once failed to do,
The same homeless you fed will put a word or two,
With all the clout he will have gained.

Blessed Be

Oh! Blessed be the day for any humble soul
To whom heavenly joys from God's mercy unfold!
When bathing in the bliss, dazzled in the rapture,
Numbed by the ecstasy, the heart's brought to flutter.
There the hypnotized gaze and the words unuttered
Beget a thrilling buzz between the ears, captured.

Oh! Blessed be this soul, right between the rhymes, caught
By a stricken writer all spellbound and distraught
Who sings eloquently of the bliss once attained,
When the soul all aglow by a most treasured mate
Trembles under a gaze! In this cold dumbstruck state,
With inner core all tamed, see the world shine, unstained!

Oh! Blessed be the soul who sets his wandering eyes
On the treasured party after much worried sighs!
There, all appeased and freed from disconcerting thoughts,
Accelerating pulse and sweaty, shaky hands,
The gratitude geysers and over the face lands
To revel in anew the embrace once so sought.

Oh! Blessed be the one, all caught in the passion,
Holding in warm embrace the chosen companion,
Sensing every heartbeat echo one's own ticker!
There, one's world may topple and fall down on its knees;
Nothing dares to mettle for gentle is the breeze
Running over one's land, restoring one meeker.

Oh! Blessed be the soul overflowing in awe
In the midst of nature, in the crude and in raw!
On a cool summer night, on a lawn, side by side,
With a myriad of stars shining down on your love,
You receive loud and clear blessings from God above
When your spirit frenzies, drunken from this joyride.

Oh! Blessed be the one, and this, many can tell,
Who on a lovely day, under clear ringing bells,
Receives the true blessings, both from heaven and earth,
To faithfully fondle the softness of a hand,
With the cutest of smile, that has forever brand'
Your heart pounding away, bursting with joy and mirth!

Oh! Blessed be the soul, in the dead of the night,
Who wakes up and discerns with ever-grateful sight
The graceful silhouette of the love of his life!
And each and every breath, sustaining her sweet soul,
Attests the blessedness that daily makes you whole
When all over the world loneliness runs so rife.

Oh! Blessed be again the soul on whom befalls
The final resonance of the expected call!
After such long mourning and hoping and praying,
After the despairing from long expectation,
Chewing the sad effect of the lack of action,
Rings in blessed sudden the voice of the darling!

Oh! Blessed be the soul, this is the final draw,
Who, thanks to the Spirit, fathoms this divine law:
To love is to suffer; it's the sine qua non
Condition of this life, if we dare to live it!
Savoring love delights comes with heavy merits
Where patient sufferings ring aloud on and on.

Daydream

If despite all efforts from the loads that I bear,
If the many concerns that erode my poor mind,
If the buzzing echo of the city's affairs
Troubles my inner peace and my poor spirit, grinds,

If again, all baffled, facing the many chores,
That make daily living so boring and so stale,
The ones that keep shackled, down to its inner core,
My soul longing to fly while I sigh and exhale.

At the least occasion, I pause just to escape
And run down the same trail that I trod yesterday.
And through this mental leap, tear down the heavy drape
Shielding this isle so fair, my treasured hideaway.

There, I run up and down its golden sand of shores;
I visit its forests, strolling under its trees.
And lost in my daydream, my spirit gently soars;
Through some magical stroke, my inner peace I seize.

Don't Cry

I hear your muttered sobs. Why are you so upset?
What's troubling your sweet soul? What worries came beset
Your fresh and tender years?
What can possibly touch such sweet and candid face?
What, in God's name, has dared your naive smile erase?
Tell me; no need to fear.

Has your dear prince charming run out of sweet nothings?
Or is that this early the disillusion sting
Burst your rosy bubble?
Then again, have your dream of Sleeping Beauty scene
Been trampled by a knight so deceiving and mean?
Please speak up; don't mumble.

I don't intend to pry but truly am concerned
To see your tender age that can barely discern
The right over the wrong
Be trampled so early by the fleeting follies
Shouted over the waves by lucky hillbillies
From the now so-called songs.

Talk to me; let it out. Often, it's a relief
To open up oneself and so pouring your grief
To a caring party.
The sadness you cling to, sealed behind your pursed lips,
Will spoil your tender mood, causing your soul to weep,
Straining your sanity.

Although some disturbance overshadows your grace
And the meaning it bears eludes your pond'ring face,
Don't give into despair.
I am here to attest that the window God seals
Is always offset by a door to make you feel
His love beyond compare.

But cry if it will help to purge your budding soul.
The failings we endure, the kindness we withhold
Summon true contrition.
The spirit will lead you to true enlightenment
And, through deep felt sorrow, cause the sincere lament,
Grace of God in action.

It's fitting that you cry in privacy as well.
Crying is like praying, and angel-ringing bells
Always bring you solace.
Hide away from the world; purify your sweet soul,
Let your tears wash the stain so to regain the whole
Loving glow of your face.

For the budding flower that in sobbing tears dawns,
With the warmth of the sun, its true colors, adorns
Lovelier than ever,
Amid dew-soaked petals and uninvited glance,
Cradles yet the courage of lovelier romance,
God's most treasured favor!

Once Upon

O my precious springtime, O sweet time of my youth!
Come, come and step right in; let us talk in all truth.
I think so much of you.
Allow for just a while that I relive the past.
Let me dive in your sets, resurrect the dear cast,
Savor you once anew.

Once when I was eighteen and with big dreams laden,
Gently lulled by my hopes that would keep me gladden,
I was upon my stage.
I lived upon my cloud, was king of my domain,
Immature to the core of which nothing remain'
Neither the lust nor the rage.

O treasured illusions, O font of dawning grace!
Of my many idylls, I recall every face,
Abrading my front gate.
Lost in the utopian, glamorous love cradle
Of which my college tasks had no business meddle,
I sprang toward my fate.

And now that life has sieved and handed me the crude,
Its essence, mirage free, its meaning in the nude;
Now morosely I tread,
Missing the early years, the once upon a time
When I was all-aglow and the star of my lime,
With clouds around my head.

What a pillage of time, what a waste of blessings!
What a painful ravage of strength, among all things,
Thought of so mournfully!
Why do we so treasure what we no longer hold?
What would I not offer to live again the old
Days of guileless folly?

When all alone, I slurp the cup of sweet recalls
You offer through the years, brewed with honey and gall,
Bringing to me your face;
The bittersweet, ever stirring, sole reaction
Brings tears to my weak sight with hints of contrition
For what I can't erase.

The blessings once bestowed on the chosen forehead,
If shunned or forgotten, will lay heavy as lead
On the bed of conscience.
They open the pouring of perpetual should-haves,
Streaming on your mind screen once-upon better-halves,
Souvenir resilience.

Please come back anytime; just come, you'll be at ease.
Come play another scene and my memory, tease.
I'll join back my writing.
My sky is overcast, and my world cold and damp.
It's warmer, cozier with the seal of your stamp
Each time my conscience rings.

Vanity, Vanity

Considering the ranks, successes, and the fame,
All thundering titles that glitter by your name,
All the sparkling and the stardom,
The loud praises bawling, the fancy church clothing,
The glamourous display of holiday nearing,
I pray the world one day, fathoms.

Hold firm to this credo that only God matters;
Hold firm to this credo: He gives life to matters.
Without His Spirit, nothing breathes.
Bullions of gold and crowns shine only one's lifetime,
But nothing He creates outshines the Great I Am,
He whose life we often deceive.

Sadly, the more we glow, the emptier we sound.
The fired torpedo becomes the big ship bound,
Not the small fish swimming its way.
Right in the hereafter, all accounts are settled;
Right in the hereafter, soul and spirit nettled
For having by us so far sway'.

Vanity, vanity, million dollars mansions!
Vanity, vanity, all the vain pretensions,
Nothing's to last under the sun.
Why all these loud gleaming when the tomb is so hushed,
Six feet away from us under hard ground or slush?
Life begins when living is gone!

Since

Since the time at hand overflows
With troubles and calamities,
Since from the horizon echoes
The rankness of insanities.

Since the elders, God bless their souls,
Blaze the trails for you to follow,
Since the children, force that unfolds,
Just like you, question tomorrow.

Since this old world from where you sprout
Sustains the source of your torments,
And that day after day you shout
Silently all wrenching laments.

Since to each step you spring forward,
One in reverse comes in response,
Since the future you look toward
Is blurred by all that you lived once.

Since the least of your source of bliss
Is tinted of pearls of sorrow,
Since a pure vessel such as this
Is neither full nor is hollow.

Since through the years of existence
The drowning doubts stifle your hopes,
Since the mirage interference
Hinders the sight of your life scope.

Since the steady chime of the clock
Brings nothing new on the table,
Since a simple walk down the block
Gets you much weaker than stable.

Transcend high above this old world,
Aspire to a higher ground,
Do not settle for its fake pearls,
Put your hopes where your heart is found.

When sadly your sun does not shine,
Focus keenly on tomorrow.
Of daily life hope is the spine,
Whereas death always rings hollow.

The shadows cater to silence
Where life is hollow and somber.
To decipher their quiescence,
Do not wake up, slumber, slumber.

The world around searches in vain
The realm of its dark dominion;
The world around remains in pain,
Lulled by its fake affirmations.

Remain steady looking ahead
And find your peace and ease your mind;
Knocking madly at every shed,
This way, soul mate you'll never find.

Fly then above the noisy flow
And set your candid pair of eyes
Way above where the heavens glow;
By God's mercy, you'll get your prize.

Evening Prayer

Come, my child, come and pray! Come, dear, on bended knee;
Come send to the heavens the substance of your plea.
The moon is all-aglow over us, the sinners,
Spreading the love of God despite all our failings.
All is said, all is done of this day expiring,
And the world retires with clothing much thinner.

The eventide lifts up the firmament curtain,
And the stars one by one their true brilliance obtain.
Through the day, we all toil, all bustle, all laden;
The stress of life's dealings throbs the heart to flutter.
To undergo repair, nature comes to shutter
Doors, minds, and all dealings. The free spirit soars then.

Now that the fallen dusk lays heavy on all lids,
It fits that all that breathes go fetch rosary beads.
For all over the world, far from creed, far from race,
Children come in and kneel, led by guardian angels,
To offer, with one voice of muted decibels,
Thanks and praises galore to the Giver of grace.

Come and pray the good Lord for your loving mother
Who through your feeble years, all your troubles smother'.
For all the lonely nights where she, with muttered voice,
Rocking with steady care your shivering cradle
And of your carry-cot steadying the paddle,
Knew to steer you away far from fright, far from noise.

Keep your father in mind. He's in much greater need.
He's so much more exposed to the snares of his greed.
But she labors firmly with her God given strength.
She listens and smoothens of her world the burdens.
Lovingly, patiently, she eases all our pains
And, with true compassion, provides care at great length.

She easily forgives and so often ignores
What, of the most common, the strong ego would bore.
The clear glow of her eyes, where naivety shines,
Can ease in any soul the deep-stirring troubles.
When her candid laughter with her sweet face doubles,
They both so silently, her blessedness, define.

So come, my lovely child. Come, your angel awaits.
Come bring to God above of your concerns the traits.
They can be so many; the world is so in need
Now that their rejection is made loud and solid.
They chose the dark pathway, where all's vile and sordid,
Worshipping their own selves and their libido, feed.

Pray for your poor father who, still weak and foolish,
Is kept yet in bondage by his own world fetish.
He's heavily laden with wants and drives galore,
And led by his vain pride, he fails to comprehend
The cold darkness at bay despite warnings at hand;
Somber bells are tolling unlike never before.

Pray for the so many who still beyond the grave,
Though they are in this world called the proud and the brave,
Are paying painfully to the divine justice
An unexpected toll for having been misled
With all the false doctrines they were sneakily fed;
Cause of that, now sadly the peaceful rest they miss.

The innocent's prayer, alms in divine basket,
Rises as the incense, all failings to offset.
Do not hold back your zest, your spirit, your ardor.
Let that everything flows from your heart to God's ears;
Tell Him of all your dreams and expose all your fears.
Delight Him the fragrance of your virtuous candor…

At the scene of her knees landing on the soft ground,
The angel of the Lord swiftly heeds every sound.
With tender attention, he transcribes and reports
The child's honest prayer. He silently remains,
Glowing his contentment, hovering her domain
Till her closing babble. Then all to God transports.

Angel of God, since you, faithfully from childhood,
Watched over night and day, much better than I could,
Every step that she takes, shield her from any harm.
Keep her under your wings, safeguard her innocence,
Save her, this is my plea, from this world's pestilence
So she reflects the glow of your angelic charm.

Sweetland

There, this is the canyon, so serene and shady,
With summer as gentle as a smooth melody.
The flowers always bloom under some lasting dew,
And the soul not clustered can ascend higher ground
Where the blissful heavens' hidden treasures abound
And man can freely meet his Creator anew.

A clear-water river, winding through its forest,
Nurtures aquatic lives where the wines grow in crest.
The meadows well heeded by some unknown tender
And the willows gathered on both sides of its bank
Seem to unceasingly, with head down, give a thank
For its ever freshness making their stalks fonder.

There, a much-needed ford reveals its rich fauna
Where peaceful fishermen run silent Daytona.
See fields of golden wheat; see streams of clear water,
See this moisture around and the cooling shadow,
The ochers of gulches and the wildlife below,
And the trees standing tall over shades and laughter.

And like a shifting crown over the green mountains,
The firmament displays all the shades it contains.
It stands as a bleu sketch of a skillful painter
Bringing to stunning life faces of jeering clouds,
Or it blinds us below with the sun high and proud
Heralding a bright moon to draw in thereafter.

It's such a unique land where your wide-open soul
Draws in from the heavens all goodness, free of toll.
I dreamed of its graces, longed for it as a child,
And would linger long while, all alone and morose,
Missing its charming scenes, in my mind all expose',
When striving in a state of young boy meek and mild.

As the day settles in, as the dusk comes to town,
After the winding trails, narrowly we come down
From the mount to the vale to reach this rustic hut
That for so long ago has been knocking the door,
The door of my daydreams, so many times before.
So hand in hand, gently, we rattle its wood, but

Thank God you are here for the door remains shut.
Not a sound, not a soul, not a wandering mutt.
Then we sit on the porch, bathing in the fresh air,
Fiddling all so gently the sweet sound of this land,
Deep in the ecstasy of this Eden at hand,
Which so connivingly would seal us as a pair.

And this charming landscape permeating so deep,
Where only the spirit its secret treasures keeps,
Impresses all around with sight, smell, and with sound.
A thicket, a willow, or a passing swallow,
A brook, or the windmill or a fleeting echo,
All that completes the sketch making this blessed ground.

Overwhelmed, quite muddled, soul-frenzied, and in awe,
We can barely recount this Sweetland that we saw.
Calmly we take the trail back to good old Stafford
Thinking about the sad and pitied condition
That we have lived thus far, skipping any mention,
Clamoring deep inside, deep, deep inside: O Lord!

Dreambound

All alone, when the sun depicts the horizon,
At this time when nature sheds its sweetest season,
The purple glare reclines, slowly fading away
While the yellow forest gold-plates all mountaintops.
The fall then skillfully, sweet nature, photoshops
As if the sun and rain rusted all on their way.

Oh! For the love of God! Who has this magic hand
That'd suddenly produce, not just only pretend,
While the shadows creep in from every known corner,
Next to me, in person, before glides in the moon,
The ever-real silhouette of my sweet Marijune
To complete this old sketch, next to me, the loner?

Let her come and instill deep within me the thrill
Of past autumn evenings, when she was the queen still.
Rekindle deep in me the love I hold so dear
While I bathe in the awe of this autumnal dusk
When in the air lingers a muttered touch of musk,
And I gaze in the thoughts of holding her so near.

Behold

Behold her smile so bright, behold her tender cheek,
Behold the newborn child so meek
With guardian angel in alert.
She favors the heavens where she came from of late,
And the duality of her fate
Shows the angel who lost her state
In this sweet child, peaceful, inert.

Behold the candid glow emerging from her eyes,
Reflecting her soul in disguise,
Still missing heavenly gardens.
Behold the transient bliss her look can hardly hide,
Revealing where she last abide':
She recently trod side by side
With the queen of celestial dens.

Behold the faint echo of angelic chorus
That gladly brought her here to us,
Of which she hears the lovely chime.
Behold the blessed sight, behold her radiant smile,
And pray that it lasts for a while,
For on this journey with long miles,
She'll miss heavens most of the time.

Summer Rain

Oh, come and see how sweet and cool
This evening turns out to be.
The morning drops from heaven's pool
Turned nature green as you can see.
The mockingbird is now tuning
While shaking water off its wings.
Soon it will find an air to mock,
Still echoing the gentle breeze
And looking for a sound to tease
Besides raindrops' steady **tok-tok**.

The steady downpour of today
Painted the sky in transient blue.
The shiny drops drenching the clay
Shimmeringly glow in a hue.
The little brook near the meadow,
For a while, in its steady flow,
Carries straw hay and fallen leaves,
Too happy to bury its bank
And playfully turned to a frank
Waterfall from a rocky sleeve.

Drifting down to the flow mercy,
Busy sharing a dead insect,
A pack of ant, from buoyancy,
Rafts far away from the whole sect
Who for the most, solidly hangs
To fallen leaves, so free of pangs

But rather enjoying the ride
Upon this, their makeshift lifeboat.
Down the brook they steadily float,
Bouncing away from side to side.

The waters made over the dune;
To the hot sun rises the steam.
In the purview, this end of June,
Nature flickers as it all seems.
Trembling are the sails in the view,
But you guess the boats though you skew,
For they appear as uncertain,
Like the shine from all the raindrops
Of glowing slate of the rooftops,
As seeing half of the mountain.

Come take a stroll on the wet land;
Inhale the healthy petrichor.
We'll go peacefully, hand in hand
Amid this riveting decor.
The sun no longer will abrade,
No need for long pause in the shade.
Come and feast on this splendid sight;
The trees, houses, and the buildings,
All in their own aspects, glowing,
Subtly heralding a cool night.

See, see the rise of dancing smoke.
Guess the rooftops under the fog.
Life is striving from divine poke;
Love in the hearts writes daily blogs.

Nature will always hit a snag
Each time sun or rain doesn't stag.
Then observe the steady decline
From the dusk hovering the town
That slowly, surely the shades drown
As the world comes in to recline.

But there comes the blessed rainbow.
See how lovely it spreads its hues.
Always after it tantrum-throws,
Heavens, of earth, kisses the bruise.
So often I wish I could fly
And size its realm in the blue sky.
But dreams are fed on its splendor,
And life takes shades in its spectrum.
But always from heavens' vacuum
Of God it reveals the grandeur.

The Bridge

Alone and dejected, I came across this path.
Alone and dejected, devoid of a mere staff.
The darkness all around fostering deadly hosts
Brought to my frightened sight some vivid scene of Faust.

I felt so despondent, so lost, and so haggard
That to the cold around I gave plain disregard.
And when in an effort I looked up to the sky,
I could only perceive far away, flickering shy,

In the distant darkness as far as eyes could see
The pale and yet shiny Godhead, the Trinity.
There the hope in my heart sprang forth and grew solid.
I thought deep in myself, eyes fixed on the pallid

Beauty in the dark sky, How can I build a bridge
And leap up off these hades? I could start on this ridge.
And with a million steps and strong beams made of steel,
I could... that's how distraught my frantic soul did feel.

And in a cold sudden, before me, with no spite,
Flickering like a ghost, dressed of the purest white,
Stood a lovely Virgin with the most peaceful poise,
Not uttering a word and inciting no noise.

Invited to do so, I followed her footsteps
And came to an abyss of which there was no depth;
Its darkness was blinding when peered at with your eyes,
And even if one tries, you could not see its size.

The fear in me grew cold; the fright choked my poor heart.
But then she looked at me and uttered, "I could start
Building a bridge for you, but you have all the tools."
And I recalled thinking, "Does she think I'm a fool?"

"We can start over here or, better yet, right there."
Then I mustered the strength to give her a good stare,
And in my trembling voice, I then asked, "What's your name?"
"You can call me Prayer. This is my claim to fame."

My most sincere gratitude to the Dover
Publications Inc. for having allowed me to dive
into their so rich collection of illustrations!

www.ingramcontent.com/pod-product-compliance
Lightning Source LLC
Chambersburg PA
CBHW021427150726
47989CB00001B/147